MW01146749

JIMMY KIMMEL

LATE-NIGHT TALK SHOW HOST

David Fischer

Enslow Publishing
101 W. 23rd Street
Suite 240
New York, NY 10011
USA
enslow.com

Published in 2019 by Enslow Publishing, LLC.
101 W. 23rd Street, Suite 240, New York, NY 10011

Library of Congress Cataloging-in-Publication Data

Names: Fischer, David, author.
Title: Jimmy Kimmel: Late-Night Talk Show Host / David Fischer.
Description: New York : Enslow Publishing, 2019. | Series: Influential lives
| Includes bibliographical references and index. | Audience: Grades 7–12.
Identifiers: LCCN 2018010349| ISBN 9781978503427 (library bound) | ISBN
9781978505179 (pbk.)
Subjects: LCSH: Kimmel, Jimmy, 1967-—Juvenile literature. | Television
personalities—United States—Biography. | Comedians—United States—Biography.
Classification: LCC PN1992.4.K48 F57 2018 | DDC 791.4502/8092 [B]—dc23
LC record available at https://lccn.loc.gov/2018010349

Printed in the United States of America

To Our Readers: We have done our best to make sure all websites in this book were active and appropriate when we went to press. However, the author and the publisher have no control over and assume no liability for the material available on those websites or on any websites they may link to. Any comments or suggestions can be sent by e-mail to customerservice@enslow.com.

3139303671 1747

Contents

Jimmy Kimmel takes the stage at the El Capitan Theater in Hollywood, where his popular late-night talk show tapes four nights a week.

Introduction

· ·

Jimmy Kimmel is in his cluttered office in the El Capitan Theater in Hollywood, California, where *Jimmy Kimmel Live!* tapes four days a week. Piles of papers and mountains of magazines tower atop his steel desk. Kimmel doesn't have many personal photos on display in the office, but there are lots of figurines, plush toys, and bobble heads lining the shelves. Two televisions are turned on: one tuned to news with the sound down, and the other showing sports highlights. It is early afternoon, so he looks less like a talk-show host and more like a hobo. He wears baggy mesh shorts, a rumpled old T-shirt, and no shoes. His hair sticks out in several different directions. A worn, brown suede sectional couch welcomes writers to come in, sit down, and pitch jokes. There's a set of bunk beds in the back from when his two older kids were young.

Kimmel watches the news to help come up with material for each night's show. He'll search and mine the internet for bits. He types ideas on his computer. He stares constantly at the screen of his laptop, siphoning through a list of nearly two hundred possible jokes submitted by every writer on his staff on a daily basis. They text last-minute punch lines for the opening monologue; his phone vibrates with the arrival of each new message. Then he begins to write, and rewrite, hone, and trim a second here, a second there. When the monologue is perfect, he gets a haircut in a barber's chair installed in a large closet across from his office. He reads the monologue to himself during the haircut, refining jokes one more time before the words are typed into a teleprompter. As he leaves the barber's chair, his transformation into a late-night star will begin.

He enters a makeup room, where a makeup artist powders his nose, plucks and shapes his eyebrows, and then applies black dye to cover the little bit of gray in his hair. In his private bathroom, he'll change into a crisp white buttoned-down shirt, knot a colorful silk necktie, and slip on gray wool-mohair Gucci pants. The wardrobe guy will bring the matching jacket, steamed and pressed. Then the staff gathers, a group of writers, producers, and technical crew, as they do before every episode, for a kind of pep rally that begins in Kimmel's office. As he makes his way downstairs, he will fist-bump everyone he passes on his way to the stage. "Best show ever!" he chants. "Best show ever!" they shout back.

Now Jimmy Kimmel is backstage at the El Capitan Theater. He peeks around the curtain to see a 250-strong crowd in the audience waiting for that night's episode to start. The band begins to play the show's theme song, and Kimmel struts onstage and into the bright lights. He hits his mark at center stage and fixes his eyes on the camera as the audience roars its welcome. It's showtime!

CHAPTER ONE

Brooklyn Boy

· · · · · · · · · · · · · · · · · · · ·

Jimmy Kimmel was born James Christian Kimmel on November 13, 1967, in Brooklyn, New York, the most populous of the five boroughs of New York City. Brooklyn is separated from the island of Manhattan by the East River and connects to the Big Apple by three bridges, one of which is the celebrated Brooklyn Bridge. Jimmy is the oldest of three children born to Joan and James Kimmel. His father, known as Jim, worked as an executive for IBM, short for International Business Machines, the largest computer company in the world, while his mother, Joan, stayed at home to care for the family. Jimmy's younger sister, Jill, was born in 1970, and a little brother, Jonathan, came along in 1976.

Jimmy was raised in the Mill Basin section of Brooklyn, a working-class, residential neighborhood surrounded by the waters of Jamaica Bay. The area used to be an industrial swampland until the 1950s, when a

Family is important to the Kimmel clan, even though Jimmy's parents, Joan and Jim, come from vastly different backgrounds.

development of more than one hundred red brick homes was constructed, each on small 50-by-100-foot (15-by-30-meter) lots. These homes featured steep outdoor cement steps leading up to a front-door entryway, which was located on the second level, with one story of living space at ground level. These modest homes all looked alike from the outside and were built very close to one another. Joan and Jim Kimmel lived in such a home at 5508 Tilden Avenue when their first child was born.

The Italian Americans of Mill Basin were proud of their homes and their Brooklyn neighborhood. The

Little Italy

New York is home to the largest Italian American population in the United States. In the late 1880s, a large number of newly arrived Italian immigrants sailed past the Statue of Liberty along the Hudson River and came through Ellis Island to start a new life in America. By 1930, New York was home to over one million Italian Americans, a whopping 17 percent of the city's population. Soon Italian immigrants dreamed of escaping the decrepit tenements and teeming streets of lower Manhattan, and throughout the early twentieth century their descendants trekked across the bridge to the borough of Brooklyn. Today, large Italian American districts are found in Brooklyn's Bensonhurst and Bay Ridge neighborhoods.

Italian community had deep roots in Brooklyn, and Mill Basin was a predominantly Italian neighborhood at the time. As such, Jimmy Kimmel was raised in a community that focused on the fundamental traditions of family, food, and faith.

Shining Example

Joan Kimmel was a doting mother who adored her firstborn son. After his birth, she started talking to Jimmy all day long and encouraged him to speak early. "He was reciting the Pledge of Alliance the day before his second birthday," his father recalled. During the years when he was an only child, Jimmy's mother tried to protect him as best she could. "Joan dressed him as John-John Kennedy with the short pants [and] knee socks—in the middle of winter in Brooklyn [when] it would be freezing out," Jim has said[1]

Jimmy's father was a shining example of the self-made man. He was a high school dropout who earned a general equivalency diploma, joined the army, and then married Joan Iacono and started a family. He worked several different jobs and then attended college. No job was beneath him. According to Jimmy, his father once worked as a short-order cook with two other men. When one cook quit, his father asked the boss if he could take over that shift to earn extra money. When the third man quit, Mr. Kimmel pocketed even more cash by taking on that shift, too.

After getting his college degree at age twenty-seven, Jim Kimmel worked his way up the corporate ladder, ultimately becoming a senior vice president with American Express before moving on to IBM's corporate headquarters in New York. The elder Kimmel worked long hours to support his family. He may have felt guilty for not spending enough time at home with his children, but Jimmy never held it against him. (As an adult, he realized how hard it is to keep a job.) The young Jimmy looked forward to occasions when he and his father spent quality time together. He especially enjoyed getting ice cream sodas with his father at the candy store across the street.

Family was important to the Kimmel clan, even though Jimmy's parents came from vastly different backgrounds. Jimmy's father was of German ancestry. Two of Jimmy's paternal great-great-grandparents were

German immigrants. One was named Konrad Kümmel. His son, Frank, who was Jimmy's great-grandfather, had a falling out with his parents, became estranged from the family, and changed his surname to Kimmel. Jimmy's father rarely talked about his German relatives. That's why Jimmy identified with his mother's side, which is the Italian side.

Jimmy Kimmel grew up in a stereotypical, large, boisterous, extended Italian family. His omnipresent relatives lived only minutes away and gathered regularly for family dinners. Jimmy's mother's brother, Vinny Iacono, and his family, and his mother's sister, Concetta, who was known as Chippy, and her husband, Frank Potenza, all lived in the neighborhood and were an integral part of Jimmy's life. "My parents . . . didn't have friends, and my aunts and uncles didn't have friends," he said. "They were each other's friends."[2]

> "My parents . . . didn't have friends, and my aunts and uncles didn't have friends. They were each other's friends."

Pass the Pasta

The Kimmels, the Iaconos, and the Potenzas shared a family meal nearly every Sunday night. The aroma of a Sunday dinner being prepared on Tilden Avenue transformed the Kimmel kitchen into an Italian restaurant. Jimmy's mother cooked all day. A potful of marinara sauce simmered on the stove while meatballs baked in the oven. Food was an essential Kimmel family

Kimmel was born in Brooklyn, New York, surrounded by a boisterous extended Italian family. His omnipresent relatives Aunt Chippy and Uncle Frank Potenza (above) lived only minutes away and were an integral part of his life.

ingredient. Any problem or challenge, no matter how large or small, was best handled over a plate of pasta. Simply put, food was their Italian penicillin.

Dinner at the Potenza home on alternate weekends followed its own familiar routine. Jimmy remembers pulling up to their house and smelling the marinara sauce from the car. At seven o'clock, Aunt Chippy served a three-course meal with platefuls of spaghetti, and after dessert her husband Frank cleared the dishes from the table and announced he was going to sleep. But Uncle Frank never retired for the night. "He was just trying to get away from everyone," Jimmy said. "Once an hour until about midnight, he'd come out of his bedroom in pajamas and [ask], 'Chippy, did you pay the water bill?' And she'd [say], 'Yeah, Frank.'" Then he would say goodnight to everyone and go back to his bedroom again."[3]

Frank Potenza was a Korean War veteran who served as a patrolman for the New York Police Department for two decades. Jimmy said his uncle arrested six people in twenty years, which made him a really good cop. "He believed a good pep talk did more good than time in jail," Jimmy said.[4] Uncle Frank also worked as a security guard at St. Patrick's Cathedral, an ornate neo-Gothic Roman Catholic church located on Fifth Avenue in Manhattan that is a tourist destination. He enjoyed talking to the visitors from foreign lands. In fact, everyone in Jimmy's family liked to talk—nonstop.

The extended family meals were an opportunity for animated conversation and debate. Jimmy's relatives were fast-talking Italians, and they yelled a lot. In fact, none of them understood the concept of whispering. They

Kimmel has two siblings: a younger sister, Jill, an actress, and a younger brother, Jonathan, who has written for six seasons of *South Park* during a time the show won three Emmy awards.

were engaging and colorful speakers, but the Kimmel family did not own "indoor voices." At the typical Sunday dinner table, the volume was somewhere around glass-shattering decibels. Dinner table discussions often became expressive outbursts, typified by loud voices, elaborate hand gesturing, and passionate arguments among family members. Eating together was a natural bonding experience, and the Sunday dinners were sacred times spent together to celebrate their blessings as a cohesive unit.

Streetwise Youth

The Mill Basin district where Jimmy Kimmel grew up was a tight-knit Italian American neighborhood. Due to the confined housing and crowded streets, they really *had* to be close. Familiar surroundings at home, at school, and at church made it easier for a shy kid like Jimmy to make friends. Like most Italian families, the Kimmels followed the Roman Catholic religion. Jimmy was baptized and made his first holy communion at St. Bernard's Church on East 69th Street. Despite growing up in a devout family of regular churchgoers, he was never one to behave like a naïve member of the Mickey Mouse Club. He and his rascal pals collected forbidden contraband and inappropriate magazines and erected a secret clubhouse to hide their cache. "We had an empty lot across the street [where] we would stash *Playboys*," he said. There were other far more dangerous capers, too. One midsummer afternoon Jimmy decided to build an enormous firecracker. He split open dozens of Roman candles and poured the gunpowder into a large tube.

Family Secret

In January 2016, Jimmy Kimmel appeared on *Finding Your Roots*, a television program that creates family trees for well-known Americans. In each episode, celebrities are given a "book of life" that traces their ancestral history through government records and public documents researched and compiled by professional genealogists. The celebrity's DNA is also tested, and a geneticist analyzes the results. The show's researchers uncovered documents showing that Kimmel's paternal great-grandfather Frank Kümmel had been born six years after Frank's parents married. Further DNA testing proved that Frank was his father's biological child with another woman. This likely explains why Kimmel's great-grandfather became estranged from his family and why he never really knew much about his father's family history.

Then he lit the fuse. "Fourth of July was like a war zone on my block," he said.[5]

Those rebellious years navigating Brooklyn's concrete jungle are some of his fondest memories. The nearby playgrounds served as gathering spots where he and his friends climbed on jungle gyms and rode seesaws. However, it was the streets, the sidewalks, the alleyways, and their front stoops that were the real playing fields of choice for Jimmy and his gang of hardscrabble friends. The neighborhood kids competed with ruthless aggression in favorite street games like stickball, punchball, stoopball, kick the can, ring-a-levio, and red rover. It was a happy Brooklyn childhood, spent in constant motion: running around the block, playing sports, building clubhouses, roughhousing with friends, and scuffling with kids from across town. "Normal kids play basketball, but we didn't have a basketball court," Jimmy said. "So we would just fight."[6]

CHAPTER TWO

Kimmel's Big Move

• • • • • • • • • • • • • •

At nine years old, Jimmy Kimmel moved with his parents, Jim and Joan, and siblings Jill and Jonathan, to Las Vegas, Nevada. The family traveled 2,500 miles (4,023 kilometers) west to escape the harsh New York winters. They settled in a home with a backyard, nestled on a rural street named Meadowlark Lane, in a quiet suburban community of the Las Vegas Valley, located in Clark County, in the southern part of the state. The valley is a 600-square-mile (1,554 sq km) basin surrounded by mountains near the Mojave Desert.

Las Vegas was a unique place to grow up. Jimmy's family lived just a few miles from the neon lights of the Las Vegas Strip—a 4-mile (6.4-km) stretch of Las Vegas Boulevard jam-packed with tourists and lined with upscale resort hotels and casinos. Today, more than forty million people visit each year, but for only a short time, to celebrate weddings and anniversaries, gamble, shop and dine, or to revel wildly at bachelor and bachelorette parties. Even though Vegas today has many more family-friendly venues than it used to, it's still a top destination for adults seeking a place to cater to sins or vices, such as lust, drinking, and gambling. Las Vegas is nicknamed Sin City because it is a top destination for all kinds of tourists looking to get away from reality and get into some trouble.

The city of Las Vegas invokes images of slot machines, alcohol, and strip clubs. The Strip is known for its carefree,

Jimmy Kimmel grew up just a few miles from the neon lights of the Las Vegas Strip, a stretch of Las Vegas Boulevard jam-packed with tourists and lined with upscale resort hotels and casinos.

anything-goes attitude. Like the city's marketing slogan says, "What happens in Vegas stays in Vegas." Of course, Las Vegas is not only casinos and cocktail lounges, and the families of Clark County, Nevada, don't live in casinos. The majority of citizens live in suburban communities surrounded by strip malls, not strip clubs. But the move to Las Vegas was a drastic change that rocked Jimmy's world. For one thing, the kids on Meadowlark Lane did not play stoopball—houses didn't even *have* a stoop.

Jimmy found himself thrown into a totally different culture. Children raised in Las Vegas do many of the same

Sin City

The population and economy of Las Vegas got a boost after World War II when soldiers and servicemen who had been stationed in the area decided to stay. Taking advantage of the economic boom, gangster Bugsy Seigel and mob boss Meyer Lansky opened the Flamingo resort and casino on Las Vegas Boulevard in December 1946. This spawned the growth of big hotels like the Tropicana and the Sands, owned and operated by known organized criminals. In the 1960s, stars like Frank Sinatra and Elvis Presley began performing at concert halls in the casinos, building a reputation for Las Vegas as the entertainment capital of the world. Las Vegas quickly became a hub for all forms of entertainment—innocent or otherwise—and if you wanted access to a vice and could pay for it, it was available.

things as kids everywhere else. They go to the movies, bowling alleys, and arcades—they just might have to walk past a casino to get there. He missed his Brooklyn neighborhood and the ice cream sodas from the candy store across the street. Now in unfamiliar surroundings, small for his age, and with a mouth as big as the chip on his shoulder, he felt like an alien in a new world. "People made fun of my Brooklyn accent," he said. "I was a little squirt of a kid, but I was quick to fight. I had to calm down and learn the ways of the West Coast."[1]

Fitting In

In many respects Jimmy Kimmel was a solitary kid. He earned good grades without really trying and displayed a distinctive artistic talent. Focused with a sketchbook in hand, he often lost himself in a private, comic book world created by his own imagination. He spent hours drawing, writing, and hand-coloring his own superhero comic books. When he was about ten, he created superhero artwork that included *The Terrific Ten*, a comic book he drew made up of characters with names like Super Duck, Lucky Lad, the Color Kid, and Muscle Man. "Color Kid was the best," Jimmy said, "because he had all the powers of the rainbow, which are really none."[2]

Slow to make friends at a new school, he indulged in minor acts of rebellion to get attention. The first time Cleto Escobedo III saw Jimmy it was a rainy day and Jimmy was riding a bicycle while wearing boxing gloves and sunglasses. Cleto was a classmate at Guinn Junior High School who lived down the street on Meadowlark Lane. The boys became inseparable. They ate lunch

Cleto Escobedo III and Jimmy Kimmel have been best friends since junior high school. An accomplished musician, Escobedo is now the bandleader for *Jimmy Kimmel Live!*

together in the school cafeteria and spent afternoons hanging out at one house or the other. Jimmy felt welcomed in the Escobedo home, but he was a shy guest and couldn't bring himself to accept a sandwich, or even a glass of water, from his friend's mother, Sylvia. Jimmy worried Cleto might think there was something wrong.

Cleto's father was a musician. Cleto Sr. made a name for himself touring in the 1960s with his band, the Dell-Kings. While working at Caesars Palace hotel and casino, he was also the personal butler to singing stars such as Sammy Davis Jr. and Tom Jones. It was common for Las Vegas parents to hold jobs in the hotels, restaurants, and casinos on the Strip, and Jimmy soon realized that family life in Vegas could be normal, with some exceptions. "Instead of 9 to 5, your mom or dad might work midnight to 8 a.m."[3]

Jimmy and Cleto soon added a third wheel, Jim Gentleman. He and Jimmy sang together in the church choir at Christ the King Catholic Community, where Jimmy was an altar boy for seven years. The three friends also bonded over their mutual admiration for a sarcastic comedian who hosted his own late-night talk show called *Late Night with David Letterman*. Letterman's appeal was his ability to mine humor from ordinary people, and occasionally their pets. He pioneered segments called "Stupid Pet Tricks" and "Stupid Human Tricks."

Letterman's brand of humor was undeniably intelligent, but also at times downright silly. He steamrolled household items and tossed watermelons off a five-story building; at one point, he wore a suit made of Velcro and jumped onto a Velcro-covered wall,

David Letterman's oddball brand of humor, such as the time he submerged himself in water while wearing a specially designed suit of sponges, was particularly appealing to a young Jimmy Kimmel.

sticking in place. (In a sequel, he wore a suit made of Alka-Seltzer and dove into an aquarium.) There were other oddball segments like the "Monkey Cam," a small camera strapped to the back of a chimpanzee who was let loose to run through the studio. Other running gags were "Top 10 Lists," "Small Town News," and "Viewer Mail."

Jimmy Kimmel thought *Late Night* was wonderfully weird and distinctively different, and he said he felt like Letterman was doing the show specifically for him. He was obsessed with the show and hosted viewing parties of *Late Night* on a black-and-white TV perched on a desk in his bedroom, the place where he used to practice his drawings. Cleto and Jim came over with sodas at

King of Comedy

David Letterman debuted as host of his nightly *Late Night* NBC television show on February 1, 1982. He later moved to CBS and hosted a combined thirty-three years, for a total of 6,028 episodes, until May 20, 2015. Letterman's run was hugely influential. He turned bizarre characters like Larry "Bud" Melman, Rupert Jee, and Biff Henderson into cult celebrities. Letterman's mother, Dorothy Mengering, also appeared on the show from time to time. In 2017, when Letterman accepted the Mark Twain Prize for American Humor, one of comedy's top honors, Jimmy Kimmel was there as a presenter. "No one from his generation influenced American comedy more," he said of his hero.[4]

midnight to watch the program while Jimmy's parents were asleep. They rarely missed an episode. "We were addicted," Jimmy said.[5]

Finding Direction

Jimmy's devotion to David Letterman went beyond teenage admiration and all the way to lifetime fan-club membership. He wore a *Late Night* letterman jacket and drew pictures of David Letterman on his textbooks in school. When he turned sixteen, his mother baked him a *Late Night* birthday cake. One year, Jimmy handed out sponges with the *Late Night* logo on them. Later, he affixed a L8 NITE vanity license plate to his first car, an Isuzu I-Mark. "I wanted to be David Letterman's friend," he said.[6]

> "**I wanted to be David Letterman's friend.**"

Letterman was television's master of the telephone practical joke. In one skit, he obtained a list of phone numbers for the offices of the company in the high-rise building across the street from his studio. Letterman dialed randomly. The first person to pick up was a young woman named Meg who willingly spoke on the air about her job. She eventually appeared some twenty times on the show, and with each appearance the gag grew more elaborate; she launched paper airplanes onto the street, tossed rolls of toilet tissue to simulate a ticker-tape parade, and lowered a phone out her window so Letterman could talk to the worker in the office below.

Jimmy watched and was amazed by what normal people were willing to do on television.

He also had a prankster's mentality, inherited from his grandfather, who enjoyed making his watch go off during the middle of church. He would also pretend to be drowning, then spit water in his rescuer's face, or lie on the floor as if he were dead until somebody found him. Another time, for no apparent reason, he wore a women's wig to a wedding and acted as if it was his real hair. To honor his family's whacky sensibility, and to emulate his television hero, it thrilled Jimmy to concoct his own outlandish pranks. He was particularly adept at phony phone calls. He spent hours prank calling strangers. Then he graduated to prank calling business owners. Jimmy ordered pizzas to be delivered somewhere unexpected. He requested taxicabs that arrived at a neighbor's address, and the frustrated driver, forced to wait for a fictitious passenger, honked the horn loud enough and long enough to wake the entire block. Eventually, the local pizza parlors and taxi vendors all refused to send anyone to Meadowlark Lane.

Jimmy Kimmel wasn't famous, but his reputation made him infamous. As a young teenager, he realized Las Vegas was a town full of magicians and blackjack dealers, and he embraced the quirks of growing up in a town where you bumped into an entertainment legend while running an errand. Jimmy once saw Liberace, the flamboyant pianist, in a hairnet at a grocery store on the Strip ordering brisket from a butcher. At fourteen, he spotted the diminutive song-and-dance man Sammy

Davis Jr. shopping for pants in the boys' department of Saks Fifth Avenue.

Las Vegas certainly is a unique place to grow up, and in a short time, it began to feel like home, a place where he belonged. Looking back, Jimmy Kimmel understood he couldn't possibly lead an ordinary childhood. "The more I describe it as a normal experience, the more I realize it was an abnormal experience."[7]

CHAPTER THREE

Merry Prankster

∙∙∙∙∙∙∙∙∙∙∙∙∙∙∙∙∙∙∙∙∙∙∙∙∙∙∙∙∙

A few years after the Kimmels moved to Las Vegas, the Potenza and Iacono families followed and moved west, too. Aunt Chippy and Uncle Frank once again were an integral part of Jimmy's life. He was also reunited with his mother's brother, Uncle Vinny, and his cousin Sal, an adolescent troublemaker four years Jimmy's junior. Now the Brooklyn relatives were together again. The large, raucous extended family dinners resumed, and a fundamental family dynamic was restored. Often, Jimmy's new friends were invited guests at the Kimmel dining room table. "It was a very entertaining family," Jim Gentleman said. "You just never knew what was going to happen."[1]

As is a common occurrence during one's teenage years, there were times when Jimmy's family embarrassed him—particularly when his pugnacious aunt argued with her husband and turned dinner into an emotional free-for-all in front of his friends. But Cleto Escobedo thought Jimmy's relatives were hilarious. He was an only child and begged to come over, just to watch the ruckus created when combative Aunt Chippy screamed at Uncle Frank. "They'd fight, but it was never mean or ugly, just funny. I loved it," Escobedo said.[2]

Inspired by David Letterman's comedy, it soon dawned on Jimmy that he could exploit his family's innate hilarity for his own amusement. He recorded family arguments and the lively conversations at the family dinner table, and then played them back for his friends. "You had to be careful what you said, because there was usually a tape recorder under the table," said his sister Jill, now an actress and writer.[3]

Jimmy was an incorrigible prankster. His favorite target was Aunt Chippy, whom he once described as being "as sweet as a shot glass full of gasoline."[4] He devised diabolical schemes to torment her and recorded her resulting tirades on tape. He collected empty soda containers and tied the tin cans to the back bumper of her car. He waited in ambush and shot at her with water guns until she was soaked through to the skin. And he planted exploding cigarettes into the pack in her purse, which detonated when she lit up to smoke. As expected, and on cue, Aunt Chippy's reactions ran the gamut from fuming indignation to incensed outrage. From Jimmy's point of view, it made for sensational comedy. He played the recordings for his friends, and they couldn't get enough.

Cleto was born with an organic appreciation for a good practical joke, too. His father used to wear a scary old-man mask around Caesars Palace, where he worked,

A Star Is Born

As a teenager, Jimmy Kimmel and his family vacationed in California. There they visited the Walk of Fame, the world-famous Hollywood landmark that honors over 2,600 celebrities in film, television, radio, theater, and music. In tribute, each luminary is awarded a five-pointed brass star embedded in the sidewalk along both sides of Hollywood Boulevard and Vine Street. At the time, Jimmy's father said to his son, "Maybe one day you'll have a star."[5] Three decades later, his father's prediction came true. On January 25, 2013, Jimmy Kimmel was honored with his own star, at 6840 Hollywood Boulevard, in front of the El Capitan Theater, where his show resides.

and scare celebrities. While Jimmy's solo shenanigans ranged from ring-and-runs to phony phone calls, when he teamed with Cleto, who was one year older, their pranks became more wicked schemes. Mr. Schilling from across the street was an unsuspecting victim. One night, he put a dead shrub at the curb for the morning garbage collection. When he awoke, he discovered the plant leaning against his front door. Mr. Schilling carried the shrub back to the curb, and the next morning, the shrub was at the front door again. This back-and-forth continued for days, and it irritated Mr. Schilling to no end. He was so annoyed that he slept on the couch in an effort to catch the culprit. He never did. Thirty years later, Jimmy and Cleto confessed to their crimes on

Kimmel's notorious pranks didn't stop once he hit the big time. In 2014, he posed as a limousine driver picking up embattled Toronto mayor Rob Ford at Los Angeles International Airport as part of a skit for his show.

national television. Mr. Schilling was surprised to learn Cleto was involved, but he always suspected the young Kimmel. "Jimmy was a terror on wheels," Mr. Schilling said. "He really tormented the neighborhood."[6]

"It Changed Everything"

Jimmy Kimmel was too shy to be the class clown, but he always has been able to make people laugh. When he was an eight-year-old elementary school student in Brooklyn, New York, a teacher told him he should become a comedian. In high school, he disrupted classes so often a teacher limited him to telling one joke a week. Despite his cut-up ways, Jimmy was a responsible student easily distracted throughout his years at Clark High School, in Las Vegas, Nevada. Outside of school he honed an admirable work ethic. He landed a job working at a clothing store on the day of his sixteenth birthday. He took a second job at a pizzeria a few months later. During his senior year of high school, Jimmy only had three morning classes and then reported to his two jobs for the remainder of the day. "I've always been a hard worker," he said. "I always had that DNA. You look to your parents and take a cue from them."[7]

His parents instilled a strong dose of self-reliance into him. They preached the value of a dollar and only grudgingly handed their son money for bowling or a movie. In fact, Jimmy hated to ask his parents to buy him anything, even brand-new clothes. "Getting a new pair of sneakers out of them was like a parable from the Bible—it was all about guilt, sacrifice and ritual," he said. By working two jobs, Jimmy earned money to spend, and the financial freedom that accompanied it. Any extra money he saved or loaned to friends. He recorded their debts in a ledger book and precisely updated the accounts each night. Jimmy took great pleasure in his newfound riches. "I never felt wealthier than when I was in high school because I was independent," he said.[8]

For much of the time he was growing up, Jimmy thought that he would become an artist or graphic designer. Every night, after his parents went to bed, he would sit at the desk in his room and draw in a sketchbook until it was very late. He kept a portfolio in which he collected his most treasured pieces. Jimmy's family expected him to pursue his talent in art. That is, until he began a lifelong obsession with David Letterman. "It changed everything," his father said.[9]

Jimmy's interest in drawing waned, and he became absolutely driven to do what he loved most: make people laugh. Though he never acted onstage in school productions, he wanted to pursue a career in comedy. He had read in a magazine interview that David Letterman had worked in radio, so he thought that would be a good place to start.

Radio Days

For amusement, Jimmy Kimmel secretly recorded prank phone calls on a tape recorder and then played them

Kimmel was honored with a star on the Hollywood Walk of Fame on January 25, 2013. As a teenager, his father had told him, "Maybe one day you'll have a star."

Honorary Degree

Jimmy Kimmel dropped out of the University of Nevada at Las Vegas in 1986 after just one year of enrollment, but the university invited him back in 2013 to award him an honorary doctorate for his television and comedic success. At the ceremony, Kimmel joked that he had worked harder on his commencement speech than on all the homework he'd had at the school. No doubt it was one of the funniest commencement addresses ever given at UNLV, but Kimmel's main message to students—finish what you started and do it well—is timeless.

for his friends. An older coworker at the clothing store worked nights at KUNV, the college radio station. He realized Jimmy was a master of the prank call and one night invited him to come on the broadcast and make prank phone calls live on the air. The jokes were a wild hit. After the show, Jimmy went home to a hero's welcome. "My parents [were] listening, my friends all listened," he said. "I got so excited by this idea of broadcasting, this idea that people could hear what I was saying. I really loved it."[10] The radio audience did, too, and the bosses at the station took notice of Jimmy's natural talent to make people laugh. They arranged for him to call in to the station a few more times after that. Pretty soon, he was given a half-hour Sunday night time slot to create a show of his own. It excited him more than anything else he had ever done. Just like Letterman, Jimmy randomly picked names from the phone book and talked to local oddballs. One guy called himself "the Hairstylist to the Stars" but admitted the only star he'd ever styled was John Davidson, a regular on *The Hollywood Squares*. "I'd goof on these people, but they were so excited to be on the radio that they didn't even notice," Jimmy said.[11]

Kimmel dropped out of the University of Nevada at Las Vegas in 1986 after just one year, but the university invited him back in 2013 to award him an honorary doctorate for his television and comedic success.

After he graduated from high school, Kimmel attended college at the University of Nevada at Las Vegas. He planned to study broadcasting, like David Letterman, but he never declared a major. As a student in high school he got good grades without really trying, but he struggled academically during his freshman year at UNLV. His overall grade point average was a mediocre 2.36 for the 1985–1986 academic year. A reason he cited for not concentrating on his studies was that the college campus was located a mere 7 miles (11 km) from his family home. "I found it difficult to pry myself away from my brother's Nintendo," he said of the video game he and Jonathan played late into the night.[12]

Extracurricular activities at the campus radio station proved a better fit than the classroom. Kimmel knew early on he wanted to be on the radio, and now he was hooked on the thrill of performing live on its airwaves. He became a minor school celebrity, but he wanted more. "I remember being a little disappointed in myself when I was 17 and I wasn't famous," he said.[13]

CHAPTER FOUR

On the Road

· · · · · · · · · · · · · · · · · · · ·

In the summer of 1986, after a year at the University of Nevada at Las Vegas, Jimmy Kimmel moved with his parents and siblings to Phoenix, Arizona. He enrolled at Arizona State University, in Tempe. The large class sizes there intimidated him, and his shyness almost became a disability. He remembered getting an F on a test because sitting in a classroom among hundreds of other students taking the same test he couldn't muster the courage to ask someone if he could borrow a pencil, having forgotten his.

Grades mattered little to Kimmel; broadcasting was all that interested him. While at Arizona State, he worked as a disc jockey at the college radio station. He also became a popular caller to the KZZP-FM afternoon show hosted by radio personalities Mike Elliott and Kent Voss. It wasn't long before Kimmel and Voss became friends. "I met him at an appearance at Houlihan's," Voss said. "He had to use a fake I.D. to get in. He was a funny guy [and] we started to hang out. His mom's a great cook and she fed me on a regular basis."[1]

Soon after Kimmel arrived in Tempe he met his first girlfriend, Gina Maddy. As a teenager, he was awkward and uncomfortable around girls, and he lacked self-confidence. Kimmel was excited to have finally met a girl who liked him and wanted to be in a relationship. He feared losing her and so did everything in his power to keep her. In 1988, Kimmel and his college sweetheart decided to marry. The news shocked family and friends. He was just twenty years old. "I was a kid. We were both very young," he said. "My mom was 19 when she got married, so it didn't seem unusual to me. It seemed unusual to all my friends, but not to me."[2]

When Kimmel got married he was forced to grow up in a hurry. He dropped out of Arizona State soon after the wedding—he'd never been all that serious about graduating—and decided to hedge his bets on a full-time radio career. "He thought [school] was useless for what he wanted to do," his mother said. Becoming a famous late-night talk-show host wasn't exactly the plan when Kimmel dropped out of college to pursue a career in radio. "He said, 'If it doesn't work out, I'll go back to school.' I figured that's all right," his father said. "He never looked back, even though there were some very shaky times."[3]

In 1989, after Kimmel left Arizona State, he landed his first paying job alongside Voss as morning-drive cohost of *The Me and Him Show* at KZOK-FM in Seattle, Washington. He and his wife packed their bags and hit

Déjà Vu

A series of pranks pulled on his bosses were the reasons Jimmy Kimmel kept getting fired. One prank bore a striking resemblance to the dead bush trick he pulled on the Schillings as a kid in Las Vegas. He found a hot dog in a boss's garbage can and put it in the boss's desk drawer. When the boss tried to throw out the frankfurter again, Kimmel put it back in his desk. The prank continued for some time. Eventually, the boss locked his office door, so Kimmel and a coprankster decided to climb in through the ceiling panels. "As I was helping my partner climb in," Kimmel said, "he fell down onto our boss's desk and just destroyed everything. We didn't know what to do, so we just locked the door and walked out."[4]

the road. It was the first in a succession of radio jobs he would be fired from over the next several years, a fate he blamed on his constant office pranks.

Stops and Starts

After he left school, Kimmel had excellent luck landing radio jobs. Holding on to them was another story. He was laid off in Phoenix, fired in Seattle and Tampa, hired in Palm Springs, lured away to Tucson, and after less than a year, fired from there, too. The same boys-will-be-boys quality of humor that made him attractive to a station in the first place would ultimately lead to his undoing. He called the boss's wife at home and on air asked personal and embarrassing questions about her husband. Audiences tuned in to listen to Kimmel's uncompromising edge, but the corporate management didn't appreciate his antics and clowning around. He secretly taped meetings when the program director was yelling at him and played back the tape on the air the next day.

When Kimmel was working at a classic rock station in Seattle just after he was married, he and partner Kent Voss were popular with the audience, and their ratings on *The Me and Him Show* rose steadily during the ten months they were on the air. But the ratings didn't matter because Kimmel mouthed off on the air about his boss, made off-color remarks, and produced scathing parody songs attacking public figures. Now the sponsors were angry, too. The last straw occurred when he used the copy machine to fabricate a nude photo of his boss and put the image on the cover of the company newsletter. Kimmel was sent packing. It was the first time he was fired, and he was devastated. "It was like a punch in the stomach. My wife and I had to move in with my parents in Phoenix. It was a humiliating experience."[5]

It took nine months for him and Voss to get another job, and their fate was repeated the following year, when WRBQ-FM in Tampa, Florida, also fired them. The unpredictable nature of radio work caused Kimmel anxiety, and money worries put pressure on his marriage, which now included a daughter, Katie. "I do remember [Gina] asking me, 'What's the plan B if this doesn't work out?' And I said, 'Just to be clear, there is no plan B. There's plan A, and that's where the alphabet ends.'"[6]

Carson Daly worked as Kimmel's intern at a Palm Springs radio station in 1993. There, he found himself forced into some truly humiliating situations as Kimmel's sidekick.

Struggling, Kimmel bounced around from market to market. He hoped to get back on his feet when he landed a spot as host of a radio show on KCMJ-AM in Palm Springs, California,

> "There is no plan B. There's plan A, and that's where the alphabet ends."

in 1992. It was there that he reconnected with Carson Daly, whom he'd met briefly years before on a church trip to Hawaii. He thought Daly was funny, so he convinced him to drop out of college in order to become his intern. With Daly as his comic foil, Kimmel's show gained notice within the industry. Soon he was poached away by a larger station in Arizona, as the morning-drive-time host at KRQQ-FM in Tucson.

The move to Tucson, Arizona, was a good career opportunity, but it upset Gina because it meant uprooting the family again. Kimmel and his wife grew distant. He felt pressured by a grueling work schedule and shouldered as much of the responsibilities of raising a young child as was possible. He worked from four in the morning until eleven in the morning. Gina worked, too. He rushed to pick up Katie from day care as quickly as he could because they couldn't afford the $5 an hour extra to keep her there longer. He'd watch her all day until six o'clock, when Gina got home. It was a hard schedule, and he was exhausted all the time. As was the pattern, just as the family got into a routine, he was fired from the job in Arizona, too, after just eleven months on the air.

Daly Beast

Carson Daly dropped out of college to become Jimmy Kimmel's intern at a radio station in Palm Springs, California, in 1993. Daly fell in love with the job, and the two became friends for life. But Daly found himself forced into some truly humiliating situations as Kimmel's radio sidekick. "He was a genius at torturing me," Daly said. Kimmel dressed his friend in a ridiculously embarrassing outfit, like a pink tutu, and then sent him outside to stand on a busy street, Fred Waring Road, at seven o'clock in the morning. Daly was "Fred" and the joke was to call in and report what Fred was wearing. "Every morning was a new adventure," he said."[7]

California Dreamin'

Kimmel and his young family, with a new addition—son Kevin—found some much-needed stability when Kimmel landed at a new broadcast home in southern California. In 1994, he joined *The Kevin & Bean Show*, a morning show on Los Angles radio superstation KROQ-FM, first as a producer and then as an on-air personality named "Jimmy the Sports Guy" who blended sports commentary and humor. A regretful joke made for a bumpy start. Kimmel stirred up controversy when he made a foolish comment on the air about African Americans and skiing. A member of the office staff, an African American known as Michael the Maintenance Man, challenged Kimmel—on air—to a boxing match for charity to settle the score. When the station put out a call for someone to train Kimmel for the boxing match dubbed "The Bleeda in Reseda" (a neighborhood in the San Fernando Valley), a fight fan and aspiring comedian listening at home knew the job was perfect for him.

Adam Carolla walked over to the radio station and got the gig training Kimmel. It probably didn't hurt that the name he dropped was Adam Lakers Carolla. His parents hadn't given him a middle name, so when it came time to get a driver's license, he chose his favorite sports team, the Lakers, and the name stuck. A close friendship formed as the two trained at a gym in Pasadena. "We worked on boxing for 20 minutes," recalled Carolla, who was then studying improvisational comedy. "Then we drank Snapple and talked about [radio shock jock] Howard Stern for three hours."[8]

Kimmel was a generous friend who championed talent. He helped Carolla get a job as cohost of the radio call-in program *Loveline* with Dr. Drew Pinsky. The show offered health and relationship advice to young adults—mixed with comedy. The show's appeal centered on the natural chemistry between Carolla, playing the role of the politically incorrect, opinionated comedian, and Dr. Drew as the nonjudgmental, authoritative physician with a reasoned clinical point of view. As for Carson Daly, he quickly moved up the ranks at KROQ-FM and within five years was the station's early evening voice. It wasn't long before he was host of MTV's smash hit *Total Request Live* and dating actresses like Jennifer Love Hewitt and Tara Reid. Daly, with his easy charm, became a teenage tastemaker in the music industry. The

Kimmel met Adam Carolla in 1994, when a Los Angeles radio station hired him to help Kimmel train for a charity boxing match. Soon after, Kimmel helped Carolla get a job as cohost of the radio call-in program *Loveline*.

NBC television network gave him a late-night talk show, *Last Call with Carson Daly*, in 2002, and then made him host of a New Year's Eve show as well. In 2011, he became a presence on prime time as host of NBC's vocal competition show *The Voice*, winner of four Emmy Awards for Outstanding Reality Competition Program in 2013, 2015, 2016, and 2017.

Watching his former protégés become famous, Kimmel wondered when, or if, he would ever get his big chance. He hustled to numerous auditions, but that breakthrough success was elusive. "I felt a little bit left behind, because both of these guys had passed me," he said. "I was always very happy for them … but it was kind of a weird thing."[9] Then Kimmel heard about a new game show that was coming to cable television, and the producers needed a host. He auditioned for the role, nailed the part of a cable television host, and got the job. That started a twenty-year chain of events that would eventually lead him on a path toward hosting the Academy Awards. Jimmy Kimmel proved that persistence is the key to success.

CHAPTER FIVE

Kimmel's Big Break

· · · · · · · · · · · · · · · · ·

When Jimmy Kimmel got married in 1988, he was just twenty years old and not emotionally prepared to be a husband. Four years later, the instincts and responsibilities of fatherhood kicked in when Gina gave birth to the couple's first child, a daughter named Katie. A son they named Kevin followed in 1993.

Kimmel dragged his wife and kids around the country as he was hired and fired from a series of radio jobs. He blazed in and flamed out mainly because he got on the wrong side of somebody.

All these different jobs helped define his work ethic, however, and he gained valuable experience in the industry. With no staff, Kimmel put together hours of material on his own. He was making $25,000 a year— not enough to support a family of four. Behind in paying bills, and terrified of being fired and forced to move his family again, he threw himself completely into the work and produced several hours of content a day. Every

Kimmel has two children with his first wife, Gina, who filed for divorce in 2003: son Kevin, pictured above with Kimmel in 2007, at the age of thirteen), and a daughter, Katie.

waking hour had to be devoted to writing material for his next show. He didn't even have time to relax and watch Letterman's show, not when he had to wake up and be at the radio station by 5:00 a.m.

Modest success at radio station KROQ-FM in Los Angeles enabled Kimmel to finally find some stability in his professional career, but he wasn't content to sit still. He aced an audition as cohost of a new television game show on Comedy Central with the offbeat title *Win Ben Stein's Money*. Kimmel was the first person to audition— and the last. "We knew we didn't have to see anyone else," said Ben Stein.[1] Jimmy Kimmel was given the job on the spot. He was going to appear on television.

Quiz Master

Win Ben Stein's Money was a game show in which deadpan actor Ben Stein competed against contestants in a satirical battle of wits. Unlike the model used by the common quiz shows, this program employed a unique concept: the contestants really were competing for Ben Stein's money. The show offered a $5,000 prize, which represented Stein's paycheck for each episode. Contestants tried to earn as much as they could, so in a very real sense contestants were taking money out of Stein's pocket.

The first half of each episode featured Kimmel as the show's announcer. Then for the second round Stein turned over the hosting duties to Kimmel and joined the three contestants in playing the game. Stein was no slouch as a contestant; highly intelligent and super competitive (especially when defending his paycheck), he regularly

Ben Stein, known for his role as the droning economics teacher in *Ferris Bueller's Day Off*, hired Kimmel to cohost a new television game show on Comedy Central with the offbeat title *Win Ben Stein's Money*.

53

trounced the other contestants and rarely gave a wrong answer, although there were a few occasions when Stein lost the entire $5,000 pot to some "superior intellect," as he would refer to that person.

Kimmel was twenty-nine with a wife and two kids, and his starting pay was just $500 an episode, not enough to justify quitting his job at the radio station. He arrived at KROQ-FM at five o'clock every morning and then drove to the Comedy Central studio to film *Ben Stein* into the evenings. It made for a punishing schedule with little time left for family. Not that Gina, in their ten years of marriage, had enjoyed much downtime with Kimmel, who describes himself as a workaholic. He's driven by ambition, to be sure, but also by the example of his mother. "She has never watched television sitting down," he said. "She will cook dinner, put it on the table and then start cleaning the kitchen. Not a moment of relaxation, and I'm exactly the same way."[2]

The allure of television was intoxicating, but exhausting. Kimmel's schedule was grueling and demanding. He developed a perpetually sleepy look and fell asleep at odd times, even in the middle of taping *Ben Stein*, which he joked was probably due to Stein's monotone speaking manner. Another time he dozed off in his car while stuck on the freeway in bumper-to-bumper traffic. He got tired every afternoon between three and six o'clock, so to keep going and stay alert he guzzled gallons of caffeinated iced tea.

Kimmel's compulsive work ethic put a strain on his family life. He was aware that his manic schedule had its costs, but he never felt compelled to tone it down.

"You have to know what you're getting into with me," he said. "I don't think it'll ever come as a surprise; you'll figure it out in the first 24 hours.

> "No one ever meets me and thinks, 'What a laid-back individual.'"

No one ever meets me and thinks, 'What a laid-back individual.'"[3]

Man Up

Win Ben Stein's Money was a critical darling and ratings hit for Comedy Central. Kimmel's quick wit and adolescent sense of humor complemented Stein's dry delivery and fake aristocratic demeanor. The combination of their personalities won the pair a Daytime Emmy Award for Outstanding Game Show Host in 1999. That year, Kimmel made the leap and left KROQ-FM to focus full-time on television work. Along with longtime friends Adam Carolla and Daniel Kellison, Kimmel established a production company under the name Jackhole Industries, Inc. The trio developed comedy shows through Jackhole and pitched them to various networks. In 1999, the company pitched one of its projects, *The Man Show*, to Comedy Central.

Carson Daly still remembers when his friend came up with the idea for the show that would become his breakout hit. Kimmel was inspired by a producer's critical comment that he would never appeal to women. So he decided to create a show that appealed to men. "We sat down, and he said, 'I'm so sick of Oprah [Winfrey] and her whole feel-good female power thing,'"

Daly said. "Then he paused and said, 'What Oprah is for women, I want to be for men. I'm going to start a show like that.'"[4] Kimmel developed a half-hour comedy show that glorified testosterone, featuring scantily clad models bouncing on trampolines, men chugging beer (sometimes while suspended upside down), and unabashed toilet humor. He recruited Adam Carolla as a gleefully politically incorrect cohost. Billed as "the anti-Oprah," the show's irreverent humor was aimed at a young male audience.

The Man Show went on the air for the first time on June 15, 1999, highlighted by flatulent chimpanzees, sexual innuendos, a lewd drinking song, and a segment titled "Cindy Crawford's Bathroom Talk" in which the supermodel displayed a surprising potty mouth. *The*

"Bueller? ... Bueller? ... Bueller?"

Ben Stein is most famous as an actor for his memorable film role as the droning economics teacher in *Ferris Bueller's Day Off* and as the monotone-voiced science teacher, Mr. Cantwell, in the hit television show *The Wonder Years*. But he is also a lawyer, professor, writer, and political commentator. He graduated with honors in economics from Columbia University and as valedictorian of Yale Law School in 1970. He worked as a speechwriter for presidents Richard Nixon and Gerald Ford and is the author of several best-selling investment guidebooks. He and Jimmy Kimmel won an Emmy Award for Best Game Show Host, surely making Stein the only economist to ever win an Emmy.

Man Show simultaneously celebrated and lampooned the stereotypical loutish male perspective in a sexually charged, humorous light. For example, the Juggy Dance Squad was a group of buxom female models that danced the shimmy in skimpy costumes at the opening of every show and in the aisles of the audience just before the commercial breaks. The program's signature sign-off segment featured sexy women in their underwear bouncing on trampolines in slow motion.

Some folks weren't laughing. Critics piled on the show. *People* magazine dubbed the premiere episode as "mostly low-class gags for guys." Kimmel described the boys-will-be-boys tone of the show as "a joyous celebration of chauvinism,"[5] and while some appreciated its anti-PC irreverence, others found it misogynistic. Common Sense Media, a trusted review guide to help families make smart TV choices, alerted parents that the show advanced a central view of women that was almost entirely negative and demeaning. "Women are almost always objectified and sexualized and are depicted as standing in the way of men, who are simply seeking the opportunity to drink beer and watch sports at their leisure."[6]

The show celebrated all that is manly, from beer to women to pornography, and though it was at times less than tasteful, it never took itself too seriously. Kimmel said the depiction of women was always intended to be tongue-in-cheek, performed along with a wink and a smile, and that no one who knew him well would ever accuse him of sexism. In any case, plenty of folks *were* laughing.

In 1999, Kimmel and Carolla starred as the politically incorrect hosts of *The Man Show*. The show celebrated all that is "manly," from beer to women to pornography, and though it was at times less than tasteful, it never took itself too seriously.

Jimmy the Italian

Jimmy "The Greek" Snyder was a Las Vegas odds maker who spent twelve years on CBS television helping football fans place their bets on NFL games. In 1996, Jimmy Kimmel became "Jimmy the Fox Guy," an on-air prognosticator doing fifteen-minute segments on Fox's Sunday NFL pregame show. Kimmel's accurate picks made him the number one sports forecaster on television, and the audience enjoyed his snarky remarks mostly directed at cohosts Terry Bradshaw and Howie Long. Although the constant ridiculing of the hosts put him in hot water with the other sportscasters, the pregame show received a distinct ratings bump during the four years when Kimmel was on, and it gave him some national name recognition when ABC began its search for a late-night host.

The Man Show was a controversial smash hit from the start. Its first raunchy episode was the highest-rated series premiere in Comedy Central history, with 1.6 million viewers. Continuing to hit new heights in infantile humor, it remained one of the highest-rated shows on cable television among males between the ages of eighteen and thirty-four during its successful run. By the end of its third season, Kimmel was pulling down $40,000 an episode.

The show's runaway success led to his frequent appearances as a commentator on *Fox NFL Sunday*, picking winners and poking fun at how seriously professional football takes itself. Now he was connecting with a larger and more diverse audience, and he was really making a name for himself. Even so, he was surprised to learn that ABC programming executives were considering him to be the host of a talk show the network was planning for its midnight time slot. Kimmel knew that *The Daily Show* host Jon Stewart was also in the running, and assumed he had no chance.

CHAPTER SIX

A Dream Comes True

· · · · · · · · · · · · · · · · · · · ·

*T*he *Man Show* trailed only *South Park* among Comedy Central's highest-rated programs and helped make Jimmy Kimmel a TV star. In the spring of 2002, the chairman of the ABC Television Group, Lloyd Braun, pitched the crazy idea of hiring Kimmel to host a talk show the network thought might have potential in the midnight time slot. He envisioned Kimmel as an irreverent new breed of host, poised to shake up an established late-night landscape with his scathing wit and proven appeal with young men ages eighteen to thirty-four, the audience most prized by advertisers. It helped that Braun's number two executive at the network was Michael Davies, who had hired Kimmel as Ben Stein's cohost. Perhaps Jon Stewart never stood a chance. In the well-reported horse race that ensued, Kimmel—fresh from the runaway success of *The Man Show*—came out in front. ABC picked him to anchor a freshly created midnight comedy vehicle called *Jimmy Kimmel Live!* At thirty-four, he had fulfilled his decades-old ambition to become a late-night talk-show host, just like his idol, David Letterman.

Jimmy Kimmel Live! debuted on January 26, 2003, with an old friend leading the band. Cleto Escobedo III had attended UNLV and then headed out on the road to perform in and around Las Vegas, where he sharpened his saxophone skills. His big break came when he joined Paula Abdul on tour, and he has since toured and recorded with Marc Anthony and Take Six. As the bandleader for *Jimmy Kimmel Live!* Escobedo performs with the Cletones, which includes his father, Cleto Sr., on horns. "I still get chills when I think back to the first night of our show," Escobedo said. "When he sat down at that desk, I was like, 'I'm watching someone's exact dream come true."[1] But Jimmy Kimmel quickly learned that fulfilling your dreams does not solve all your problems.

As his television career was just getting started, his home life, never perfect, had gone to shambles. He and Gina's marriage soon dissolved. The couple separated in 2002, and the fourteen-year marriage officially ended when Gina formally filed for divorce in June 2003. Each parent continued to share custody of their two children, who both went on to attend college near Chicago (Katie studied art, while Kevin studied filmmaking), but Kimmel and his ex-wife are not on good terms, and he does not like discussing his first marriage publicly.

He reacted to the stress of his divorce by channeling the anxiety into work, and he soon gained a reputation for being unusually involved in the nitty-gritty details of his new show. Kimmel's show went on the air at midnight, one half hour after NBC's *The Tonight Show with Jay*

Jimmy Kimmel Live! made its television debut on January 26, 2003. At 34, Kimmel had fulfilled his decades-long ambition to become a late-night talk show host like his idol, David Letterman.

•••••••••••••••••••••

Leno and CBS's *Late Night with David Letterman*. He competed against the two titans of late night and gave away a thirty-minute head start. If *Jimmy Kimmel Live!* was to be a success at midnight, viewers needed to make a conscious choice to switch channels.

In the quest for ratings, Kimmel decided to go after Leno's audience. Leno had once disrespected Letterman, so Kimmel loathed him. He fired the first salvo by saying he intended to do "the comedy version of *The Tonight Show*."[2] He scorned Leno with a mocking impersonation— gray backcombed wig and jutting prosthetic chin— and in an exaggerated high-pitched voice he delivered purposefully corny jokes that produced groans from the audience and sarcastic rim shots from the drummer. "As a comedian," he said of Leno, "you can't not have disdain for what he's done: He totally sold out."[3]

Kimmel did his show live—at least for the first year—from Hollywood's ornate El Capitan Theater before an audience treated to an open bar. He wanted a show with a more casual, raucous vibe than the ones produced by Letterman and Leno. Mission accomplished. To the audience's delight, Kimmel filled the show with man-on-the-street pranks, and he insulted Oprah Winfrey constantly. He also invited rapper Snoop Dogg and former boxer Mike Tyson to cohost for a week during that first season, to mixed results and mixed drinks.

Perfect Match

Behind-the-camera pursuits blossomed for Kimmel as well, and extra energy went into Jackhole Industries, the production company he had started with Adam Carolla and Daniel Kellison. The company's mascot is a donkey wearing a sombrero. In 2002, the team created a popular show called *Crank Yankers*, which aired on Comedy Central. Other shows followed, such as the *Sports Show with Norm Macdonald* and *The Andy Milonakis Show*.

Crank Yankers stemmed directly from Kimmel's childhood imagination. The show made all the crank phone calls he wished he'd made when he was a kid. There's something nostalgic about crank phone calls. They're the product of a bygone era, and if you were born before the invention of Caller ID, they were likely a part of your childhood.

Some of the biggest stand-up comics, including Tracy Morgan and Jim Florentine, joined Kimmel and Carolla to make prank phone calls and voice the *Crank Yankers* puppets.

On *Crank Yankers* comedians made real prank phone calls to unsuspecting people and recorded the hilarious conversations. Then puppets, the citizens of Yankerville, gave visual support and reenacted what was happening on the phone calls. Some of the biggest celebrities in stand-up comedy, including Dave Chappelle, Sarah Silverman, Tracy Morgan, and Dane Cook, made the calls and voiced the puppets. A total of seventy episodes were produced. Kimmel voiced the character of Elmer Higgins, a crabby, elderly man based on his grandfather. Elmer Higgins made complaint calls and frequently went off on long-winded tangents about his younger days.

Child Labor

Jimmy Kimmel voiced several puppet characters on *Crank Yankers*, including a grown man named Jimmy that lived with his mother. Jimmy was the father of two young children that lived there, too. The children played juvenile pranks and used inappropriate foul language. Kimmel's kids, Kevin and Katie, voiced these children on a few episodes during the 2003 season. He claimed his son and daughter are not particularly foul-mouthed in real life. "My definition of cursing is probably different from what other people's definitions are," he said. "But I wouldn't ask them to say anything I don't hear them say already."[4]

Once he tried to make an appointment to get hearing aids over the phone, which went terribly wrong.

Kimmel became closer to friend and *Crank Yankers* costar Sarah Silverman and the two became involved in an off-screen, on-and-off-again relationship. "We first met at the Hugh Hefner Friars Club Roast," she said. "Jimmy was the host and I was a roaster. He said I was a slut and I called him fat and charisma-less."[5] The two were an almost-perfect match. They began dating shortly thereafter, making a sweet team that had an unusual penchant for sharing personal details in a highly public way. Kimmel and Silverman briefly split in July 2008, and after reuniting later that year, the hip and funny duo got back together briefly, only to break up a second and final time in March 2009.

Shortly after the breakup, Kimmel made a TV appearance on *The View* dressed as former panelist Rosie O'Donnell. He wore a wig, stretch pants, and a blouse. Asked why the relationship with Silverman ended, he replied with a reference to his costume, "What do you mean, what happened? Look at me. What do you think happened? I'm a 41-year-old man with a bra filled

Kimmel and then-girlfriend Sarah Silverman were an almost-perfect match. They dated for several years, making a sweet team that had an unusual penchant for sharing personal details in a highly public way.

with Koosh balls. I'm an imbecile. She couldn't date an imbecile anymore."[6] Kimmel and Silverman remained close friends. When she appeared on *Jimmy Kimmel Live!* in November 2013, she came armed with a box that contained her ex-boyfriend's belongings and returned them to him.

Sleeper Star

Going nonstop at a hectic pace, Kimmel noticed that the caffeinated iced tea he drank no longer kept him going. He got very tired every afternoon during the writers' meeting, so he finally decided to see a doctor. The doctor was concerned that he might have narcolepsy, a neurological sleep disorder. All Kimmel knew about narcolepsy was a character on the television show *Hill Street Blues*, Vic Hitler the Narcoleptic Comic, who fell asleep in the middle of his act. The doctor diagnosed Kimmel with a mild case of the disorder and prescribed a medication called Provigil. Only in recent decades have doctors come to better understand narcolepsy, and therefore for years its symptoms went undiagnosed. Historical figures who possibly had narcolepsy include Winston Churchill, the former British prime minister; Thomas Edison, the inventor of the lightbulb; Harriet Tubman, the abolitionist who helped many slaves to freedom; and Louis Braille, creator of the reading system for the blind known as Braille.

> I'm an imbecile. She couldn't date an imbecile anymore.

The Drowsy Comedian

Jimmy Kimmel went public as a narcoleptic in 2003. Narcolepsy is a neurological sleep disorder in which the brain loses its ability to maintain normal sleep and wake states, causing excessive sleepiness and frequent daytime sleep attacks lasting from a few seconds to several minutes. In rare cases, sleep attacks extend for an hour or longer. Statistics indicate that the sleeping disorder affects as many as two hundred thousand people in the United States and approximately three million people around the world. There are no quick fixes for narcolepsy, since doctors don't truly understand it and therefore can't cure it.

Kimmel announced to the public that he was a narcoleptic in the August 2003 issue of *Esquire* magazine. He published an essay titled "What It Feels Like to Have Narcolepsy." In it, he joked that being narcoleptic was the best thing to ever happen to him because he can board a flight to Vegas and fall asleep before the plane takes off and wake up after it's landed. He went public about being a narcoleptic to raise awareness about the malady, though he acknowledged that being known as Jimmy Kimmel the Narcoleptic Late-Night Comedian has a certain weird, circus-sideshow ring to it. When asked if he would ever be the public face of narcolepsy, he said, in typical self-disparagement, "No. Nobody wants me associated with their group."[7]

CHAPTER SEVEN

Kimmel Hits the Big Time

· · · · · · · · · · · · · · · · · · ·

Television hosting did not come naturally to Jimmy Kimmel, and neither did an audience. His first guest on *Jimmy Kimmel Live!* was the A-list actor George Clooney. Although he had been a radio host for years, Kimmel still had a lot to learn about being a good television host. In the first two seasons, he seemed to portray a friendly loudmouth crashing the late-show party. He was often unprepared and asked few questions of interest. In his eagerness to be distinctive, questionable moves were made. Kimmel thumbed his nose at many of the expected time-honored talk show customs: He refused to wear a necktie, scrapped the traditional opening monologue, and served unlimited quantities of wine and liquor to the audience.

Despite the show's edgy content, ratings were mediocre and reviews were worse. Nancy Franklin, the *New Yorker* TV critic, called the show "dead on arrival" and said its host should be "admitted immediately to the Witless Protection Program."[1] There were occasional flashes of zany brilliance, like the popular recurring comedy segments "Celebrities Read Mean Tweets," in which celebrities read aloud the insulting comments written about them on Twitter, and "This Week in Unnecessary Censorship," in which innocuous words were bleeped out of video clips as though they were

One of the most popular comedy bits on *Jimmy Kimmel Live!* is the recurring segment "Celebrities Read Mean Tweets," in which celebrities like Robert De Niro read aloud the insulting comments written about them on Twitter.

profanities. But Kimmel had a difficult time booking guests, especially women. After the first six months, he was hoping the show would get canceled.

Network executives urged Kimmel to dull the rough edges. He listened to their advice and accepted the conventional wisdom. He dieted and lost twenty pounds (9 kilograms). He wore neckties and did an opening

monologue. Liquor was no longer served to audience members. Kimmel worked hard to shed the frat-boy image he had established as a host of *The Man Show*. He even got a sidekick, Guillermo Rodriguez, a former parking lot security guard with a natural comedic gift. The Mexican American's broken English causes him to pronunciation his boss' name as "Yim-ee." Rodriguez frequently serves as the show's celebrity gossip

Guillermo Rodriguez, Kimmel's sidekick on *Jimmy Kimmel Live!*, is seemingly game for anything Kimmel throws at him.

correspondent in the popular segment "Guillermo's Hollywood Round-Up."

Family Ties

Many comedians portray themselves as tortured types with miserable childhoods that want to escape their families. Kimmel, by contrast, surrounded himself with relatives. In a way, they're his secret weapons. His brother, Jonathan, works as a segment director on the show after three years as a writer on the program. His writing credits include six seasons of *South Park* during a time the show won three Emmys. Cousin Sal Iacono joined the writing staff of *Jimmy Kimmel Live!*

Hoop Dreams

For the past several years, *Jimmy Kimmel Live!* has sent Guillermo Rodriguez to media day at the NBA Finals. Standing at 5'4" (162 centimeters), when Guillermo interviews basketball players he is easily dwarfed by them, so he stands on a stepstool to make himself look taller. He has interviewed stars like Stephen Curry and Kevin Durant, but he's never scored an interview with LeBron James. In 2017, Rodriguez turned the tables on LeBron. He told every player he interviewed to tell LeBron that he wasn't talking to him, hoping that LeBron would change his mind, but he never did. During the game, whenever LeBron ran by on the court, Rodriguez yelled at him, "Hey LeBron, I'm not talking to you!"

in 2003. He is featured in several recurring bits, many of which involve pranks that he played as a child. He also appears frequently on the show in hidden camera comedy sketches in which he pretends to be a store employee or a delivery person who is incredibly inept or annoying.

Aunt Chippy is a foulmouthed regular on the show, and Kimmel gets a kick out of exploiting her gullibility. In one of the most unbelievable April Fools' Day pranks ever, Kimmel and his cousin Sal set up a fake sonogram appointment with a fake sonogram technician at a real sonogram facility for their pregnant cousin, Micki. She was in on the bit, and she invited her unsuspecting mother (Jimmy and Sal's aunt Chippy) to come along to see the baby. Aunt Chippy had never seen a sonogram before. What she saw was definitely a surprise. A few weeks before, Kimmel had the show's graphics department give the baby in the womb a little extra life. The result: a hand-clapping, nose-picking, booger-eating, middle-finger-flipping, and jig-dancing baby. To Aunt Chippy's astonishment, the sonogram showed the mother-to-be was actually expecting twins—one that resembled Cousin Sal and the other that looked like Jimmy! Aunt Chippy's reaction was priceless.

Kimmel's brassy Aunt Chippy, whose real name is Concetta Potenza, was married to Frank Potenza for twenty-eight years. The two divorced in the mid-1990s and remained very close friends. Chippy currently lives in Las Vegas and works in collections for a company that provides vitamin supplements. Kimmel said his finest hour was when he hired a bunch of actors pretending to

Cousin Sal Iacono (at left, pictured with Guillermo, Jimmy, Aunt Chippy, and Uncle Frank) joined Kimmel's writing staff in 2003. He is featured in several recurring bits, many of which involve pranks that he played as a child.

· ·

be painters, and also pretending that they didn't speak English, to paint Aunt Chippy's house orange and green while she was at work. They even painted the trees in her yard. She came home from work and started yelling at the workers, demanding to know what was going on. And none of them spoke English, which made her madder and madder. Then a painter handed her a beer and she went crazy and threw the can of beer at him.

All the Kimmels, Iaconos, and Potenzas bring out the best in Jimmy, sometimes with sidesplitting results. Uncle Frank was a retired Brooklyn cop who figured into numerous on-camera bits. Uncle Frank wore a security uniform, and Kimmel always identified him as the show's security guard. That was a job Mr. Potenza was well qualified for. He provided security at St. Patrick's Cathedral in New York for a time, and later he worked for twenty years as a security guard for Caesars Palace in Las Vegas, where his clients included Frank Sinatra. As a comic foil to his nephew, Uncle Frank put his own signature on each assignment. He would in-line skate, let his head be shaved, wear any costume, and say anything to anybody. His red carpet interviews with Meryl Streep and Tom Cruise, which left both stars speechless, underscored the satiric absurdity that Kimmel clearly felt Uncle Frank brought to the table. In one of his funniest moments on the show, Uncle Frank had a long conversation backstage with Kermit the Frog, a Muppet from *Sesame Street*, discussing romances gone bad (Uncle Frank's ex-wife versus Miss Piggy), with Uncle Frank accepting Kermit's experiences as just as real as his own.

Human Touch

When Frank Potenza died in August 2011, Kimmel delivered an emotional tribute to his uncle. He choked up when he told viewers stories about how Potenza never wanted to be late for the show and in fact would show up ten hours early for the show's taping. "It's hard to believe he's now the 'late' Uncle Frank because he was never ever late for anything," Kimmel said.[2] Potenza was 77 when he died, and Kimmel joked that he had planned to live to 103, just to stick the city with another

Trick or Treat

Jimmy Kimmel is known for his easy rapport with children, but he has made it his mission to temporarily torture them on Halloween. Since 2010, he has asked parents to fake-out their kids by telling them that they ate all their Halloween candy and then post video of their reactions to YouTube the morning after the sugar-filled holiday. The show received over one thousand videos in 2017, and it turned out there are a lot of parents in the world who are willing to prank their children and face the consequences, including the case of one kid who threw a punch. There were tears, tantrums, an accusation of being "selfish," and one particularly upset youngster who announced, "That's why I don't love you anymore."[3]

twenty-five years of pension checks. Then he played a video montage of Uncle Frank's greatest moments on the show, with a recording of Frank Sinatra's *My Way* as the soundtrack. The montage ended with Uncle Frank singing the last line of the song, painfully off-key and out of tune, which was the point of the joke. He couldn't sing and he didn't care.

It's a good thing the network trusted Kimmel's instincts and gave him a long leash because it took a while for *Jimmy Kimmel Live!* to catch on. Gradually, the show attracted a solid core of enthusiastic followers. He could make people laugh, but he also showed a sentimental side and an emotional vulnerability that viewers found refreshing. Kimmel had succeeded in his attempt to better connect with the audience. He started out as a caricature, but now he was a real person with real human feelings. He downplayed the more belligerent, acerbic persona he'd cultivated on *The Man Show* and *Crank Yankers* and began showcasing softer sides of himself, like his easy rapport with children. Eventually he even had Oprah Winfrey on as a guest and engaged in a "nice-off" with Ellen DeGeneres, battling to see who could out-compliment whom. (Kimmel lost, but it was close.)

> I never want to think of myself as a fixture.

The show had been slow to take off, but Kimmel steadily built a loyal viewership and eventually carved out a place for himself in the late-night history books. *Jimmy Kimmel Live!* now pulls in a nightly audience of over two million viewers, and Kimmel himself is now fully cemented as a fixture in the pantheon of late-night television hosts. "I never want to think of myself as a fixture," he said. "A faucet is a kind of fixture. A fixture is something you count on because you can forget it."[4]

CHAPTER EIGHT

Kimmel
Goes Viral

• • • • • • • • • • • • • • • • •

J immy Kimmel has an uncanny ability to craft bits that are all but guaranteed to go viral on the internet. His YouTube channel had over 11 million subscribers and boasted over 5.6 billion views as of February 2018. His show has been particularly adept at cranking out video sketches designed to thrive outside of the traditional broadcast format, like the time on Valentine's Day 2013 when he put actress Jessica Alba inside a glass-encased kissing booth on the street outside the studio. That video clip alone has nearly 5 million views. Despite his digital savvy and online marketing success, Kimmel points out, "We're not in the business of making viral videos. We're in the business of making a television show."[1]

Yet Kimmel has adapted well to the digital age, and his comedy that plays well on the air also has a second life on the web. In January 2008, Sarah Silverman appeared on *Jimmy Kimmel Live!* to show Kimmel, her boyfriend at the time, a special video as a surprise for his forty-first birthday. The video turned out to be a song called "I'm

F*@#ing Matt Damon," in which she and Matt Damon sang a duet about having an affair behind Kimmel's back. The video went viral and created an instant YouTube sensation that has been watched more than 19 million times. Silverman won an Emmy Award for outstanding music and lyrics for her efforts.

Kimmel responded with his own video one month later with Damon's friend Ben Affleck and a group of megastars to record Kimmel's song of revenge, "I'm F*@#ing Ben Affleck," which has nearly 13 million views. The two are seen giving each other pedicures and then Affleck pinches Kimmel's bare chest. It wasn't just a duet; it was an all-star performance on par with "We Are the World." Kimmel's backup singers included a who's who of the entertainment industry, including Don Cheadle, Cameron Diaz, Huey Lewis, Christina Applegate, Joan Jett, Macy Gray, Lance Bass, Josh Groban, Ashlee Simpson, and Harrison Ford, who blows the new couple a kiss. Even Brad Pitt made a cameo appearance as a FedEx deliveryman who brings a cake of congratulations to Kimmel and Affleck, who stand nose-to-nose in the video and very nearly kiss. A breathless Robin Williams gushed, "This is not a man crush."[2]

A long-standing "feud" that had developed between Kimmel and Damon now reached a boiling point. In 2013, Damon took over an entire episode of *Jimmy Kimmel Live!* as a maniacal supervillain who hogtied Kimmel backstage and was determined to overthrow the show. The following year, Damon was invited as a guest on the show with the cast of *The Monuments Men*. However, Kimmel never asked Damon a question, and when he finally got around to doing so, the fire alarm mysteriously sounded before Damon could answer. The duo eventually attempted to work through their differences in a session of couples counseling in 2015, but it was unsuccessful.

Kimmel and Damon have been fake feuding for over a decade, and no occasion is too fancy for the frenemies' constant bickering. While hosting the 2017 Academy Awards, Kimmel needled Damon during the opening monologue, calling the actor an idiot who turned down the chance to play an Oscar-winning role in *Manchester by the Sea*, which Damon produced, by handing the role to his friend Casey Affleck so he could be available for "a Chinese ponytail movie instead. And that movie, *The Great Wall*, went on to lose $80 million."[3] Damon responded to the insult by attempting to trip Kimmel as he walked through the aisle. Then, as a lead-up to

Kimmel and actor Matt Damon have been fake feuding for over a decade. It all began during the third season of *Jimmy Kimmel Live!* when the host off-handedly ended a disappointing show by apologizing to Damon for bumping him from the episode.

Damon presenting an award, Kimmel aired a pre-taped clip in which he reminisced about seeing the actor's 2011 film, *We Bought a Zoo*, in a completely empty theater. "The thing about Matt is that you can see how hard he's working, it's so effortful for him," Kimmel said.[4] Later, Damon and Kimmel stared warily at each other when their paths crossed onstage, when Damon presented an award and Kimmel tried to play him off the stage with swelling music by personally conducting the orchestra to do so.

Favored Host

Jimmy Kimmel seemed to be everywhere in 2012. There he was at the White House Correspondents' Association Dinner, which he hosted in April, getting a big laugh when he said, "If you told me when I was a kid I would be standing on a dais with President Barack Obama, I would have said, 'The president's name is Barack Obama?'" He spent the rest of the evening poking fun at politicians like Newt Gingrich, the puffy, pear-shaped former Speaker of the House. "Mr. Gingrich, how can you be against gay marriage," Kimmel asked, "when you yourself are the child of a gay marriage: the Michelin Man and the Stay Puft Marshmallow Man?" He also gave extra attention to New Jersey governor Chris Christie, focusing on the governor's weight. "You might be misunderstanding the New Jersey state slogan," Kimmel cracked. "It's not the Olive Garden State." At the end, Kimmel dissed his tenth grade history teacher, Mr. Mills, who said he'd never amount to anything if he kept screwing around. "I'm about to high-five the president!"[5]

Kimmel continued to sharpen his hosting chops, next at the Emmy Awards, which he hosted in September, where he punked the format in novel ways like running an "In Memoriam" segment set to a stirring Josh Groban accompaniment and devoted entirely to clips of Kimmel himself. Kimmel has since become a regular presence as an awards show master of ceremonies. He hosted the Emmy Awards twice, in 2012 and again in 2016 to positive reviews, the American Music Awards five times, and the ESPY Awards with LeBron James on ESPN. Kimmel also served memorably as emcee for Comedy Central roasts of Hugh Hefner, Pamela Anderson, and Flavor Flav.

Internet Sensation

The infamous feud between Jimmy Kimmel and Matt Damon may not be real, but it sure is entertaining. It all began during the third season of *Jimmy Kimmel Live!* when the host off-handedly ended a disappointing show by apologizing to Damon for bumping him from the episode. After the joke got a big laugh, he repeated it every night. "We had a bad show [and] I decided to say, 'I want to apologize to Matt Damon. We ran out of time.'"[6] Kimmel went on to explain that Damon was just the first name that popped into his head. He was trying to think of an A-list star, somebody the show absolutely would not bump. Since its inception, the bit has evolved from an improvised one-liner to a series of elaborate segments, resulting in one of the most enduring late-night gags ever.

Kimmel got big laughs as host of the White House Correspondents' Association Dinner in 2012. He spent the evening poking fun at politicians, and at the end, high-fived President Barack Obama.

● ● ● ● ● ● ● ● ● ● ● ● ● ● ● ● ● ● ● ●

In 2017, Kimmel, forty-nine, hosted the Academy Awards ceremony for the first time. The selection of Kimmel by the Academy of Motion Picture Arts and Sciences to preside over the conservative and sometimes stuffy Oscars telecast proved how far he'd come in resurrecting his image and earning the respect of his peers in the television industry. Ironically, reporters called Kimmel "a boring, perfect choice" and praised the Academy for "playing it down the middle with its controversy-free choice of Kimmel as Oscars host."[7] He was comfortable and confident during the show and was lauded for keeping cool when the broadcast nearly collapsed into chaos after the Oscar for Best Picture was mistakenly given to the wrong film due to a mix-up with the envelope. It was a prank not even Kimmel could make up.

"I'm about to high-five the president!"

During the fiasco, he came on the stage and jokingly took responsibility. "I knew I would screw this show up," joked Kimmel, who was not the one who screwed up. "I promise I'll never come back."[8] As it turned out, when he hosted again in March 2018, he became the first person to host back-to-back Oscars since Billy Crystal did the honors in 1997 and 1998.

Charity Cases

Jimmy Kimmel is involved with several worthy charities. In September 2017, he was among the celebrity food lovers that helped raise more than $1.3 million to fight pediatric cancer at a fund-raiser for Alex's Lemonade Stand Foundation, a leading nonprofit organization. Perhaps his favorite cause is the San Gennaro Foundation, host of the Feast of San Gennaro, which celebrates Italian culture through entertainment, music, and cuisine. The festival is an annual tradition of his New York Italian Catholic heritage. In 2002, Kimmel and Adam Carolla brought the Feast of San Gennaro to Los Angeles, and the festival, complete with a mass and procession through the streets, honors outstanding members of the community and raises funds to aid disadvantaged children and needy families in the city.

Late-Night Wars

The culmination of Kimmel's decade-long evolution arrived in August 2012, on the eve of his show's tenth anniversary on air, when it was announced that the ABC late-night show would move to the coveted 11:35 p.m. timeslot. The decision to move the show to an earlier start time would put *Jimmy Kimmel Live!* in head-to-head competition with NBC's *The Tonight Show with Jay Leno* and CBS's *Late Show with David Letterman*. The announcement came as host Kimmel, forty-four, was given a two-year contract extension, and soon after, for the first time his program was nominated for an Emmy Award in the late-night variety show category.

Kimmel finally got to interview his idol, David Letterman, when Letterman appeared as a guest on Kimmel's show during a broadcast from Brooklyn on Halloween night, October 31, 2012. Kimmel told Letterman he was the main reason he got into television. To prove what a fan boy he is, Kimmel pulled out pictures of himself as a teenager blowing out candles on a Letterman-inspired birthday cake and of his car, with its L8 NITE vanity license plate. Letterman was gracious about Kimmel's show moving to the same time slot and offered his blessing. "I want to wish you the best of luck when you move the show," he said. "I think you're going to be perfect at 11:30."[9] Kimmel's broadcast from Brooklyn the week after Hurricane Sandy ended up being the second most watched week in the show's history.

Jimmy Kimmel Live! made an impressive debut in the new 11:35 p.m. timeslot on January 8, 2013, beating

As host of the 2017 Academy Awards, Kimmel was praised for keeping his cool when the broadcast collapsed into chaos after the award for Best Picture was mistakenly given to the wrong film.

● ● ● ● ● ● ● ● ● ● ● ● ● ● ● ● ● ● ● ●

his idol David Letterman in the ratings and falling just short of his rival Jay Leno. The premiere at his new time yielded Kimmel his second-biggest audience ever, with 3.1 million viewers, according to Nielsen ratings. That put Kimmel slightly behind Leno, with 3.3 million viewers, but ahead of Letterman's 2.9 million viewers. Jennifer Aniston helped Kimmel christen his new timeslot as his first guest. She entered the stage wielding a sledgehammer and wearing safety goggles and work gloves, and she proceeded to smash to bits what she thought was Kimmel's old desk. "Out with the old, in with the new, we're going to 11:30!" Aniston proclaimed. She apologized when informed by Kimmel that that was his *new* desk and then gave him a haircut.[10]

Jimmy Kimmel has hosted thousands of episodes since his late-night show's premiere, and he has finally earned the respect of A-list guests and beaten out rival late-night talk shows in the ratings. Over the show's decade and a half run, ABC has repeatedly extended Kimmel's contract at an annual salary reported at $10 million due to his continued success as host of *Jimmy Kimmel Live!* He has invested some of his riches into building a home life that allows him to enjoy getting away from the office. His Sunday afternoon football parties for 100 to 150 people have become the stuff of Hollywood culinary legend. On the patio at Kimmel's Hollywood home, near a fire pit, swimming pool, and miniature waterfall, he's installed a wood-burning pizza oven. It sits beside a smoker, a barbeque grill, a tandoor oven, and a paella grill. A cooking enthusiast, Kimmel grows fresh herbs and he makes his own vinegar.

Kimmel's sensitive and nurturing side is evident in his involvement with several worthy charities. In January 2013, he requested monetary donations to benefit Comfort the Children International, a community of people working diligently to create solutions and opportunities for a better life for children in Kenya. By donating at least $33 to Kimmel's campaign, people were entered in the chance to win tickets to *Jimmy Kimmel Live!* in Hollywood. And if that wasn't enough, donors also won the right to have Kimmel punch a friend of their choice in the stomach. That's right. Punch a friend in the stomach—for the benefit of children!

CHAPTER NINE

A New Leaf

· · · · · · · · · · · · · · · · ·

Jimmy Kimmel's drive and single-minded focus are legendary. For instance, back in October 2007 he earned a Guinness World Record for Furthest Distance Commuted in One Working Week when he served as both guest cohost on *Live with Regis and Kelly* in New York City and host of his own show in Los Angeles. Kimmel's feat was remarkable. In the process, he traveled a total of 22,406 miles (36,059 km) in a single working week. His daily commute was back and forth across the country, cohosting live with Kelly Ripa in New York each morning and taping his own show in Los Angeles each night. That's two cross-country flights a day for five days in a row. "I am a little bit insane," he said. "People can tune in and watch me collapse on air."[1]

Even now, Kimmel has a hard time keeping still. It's fitting that in his office at the El Capitan Theater he uses a treadmill desk and walks at a brisk 4 miles (6.4 km) per hour as he answers e-mails, reviews the news of the day, and puts the finishing touches on the monologue for that evening's show. Kimmel is perpetually in motion, always on the go, looking forward to the next project, and ready to take on new challenges. "It's hard for me to enjoy the moment," he said. "I'm thinking about not failing. It's an anxious way to live, and it makes me feel guilty when I'm relaxing."[2]

Office Romance

In October 2009, Jimmy Kimmel started dating Molly McNearney, a co-head writer who had worked for

Over the decade and a half *Jimmy Kimmel Live!* has been on the air, ABC has repeatedly extended Kimmel's contract due to his continued success as host of the late-night show.

the show almost since its 2003 debut. She started as a writer's assistant and rose steadily through the ranks. Kimmel was attracted to the tall, athletic woman with dirty-blond hair and a sly smile. At one of the writers' meetings, Kimmel asked everyone to list their five favorite foods. McNearney named pizza, gnocchi, crab claws, a BLT, and a cheeseburger. Soon after, Kimmel invited her to dinner at his house. He cooked crab claws, a pizza, a BLT, a cheeseburger, and gnocchi, all from scratch. That sealed the deal, McNearney said, as she realized how incredibly thoughtful and generous he was.

In August of 2012, Kimmel, forty-five, proposed to McNearney, thirty-five, while the two were vacationing in South Africa. They wed on July 13, 2013, in Ojai, California, and recited their own vows before a cadre of celebrity guests that included Jennifer Aniston, Matt Damon, Ben Affleck, Jennifer Garner, Ellen DeGeneres, Stanley Tucci, Howard Stern, Kristen Bell, and Dax Shepard. At the wedding ceremony, McNearney pranked Kimmel by getting actress Gabourey Sidibe to stand in for her and surprise Kimmel by walking down the aisle in a replica of her white wedding dress. No one knew of the prank, not even her parents. When the *Precious* star appeared, McNearney's dad said, "Oh no, someone double-booked!"[3] Not wanting to steal the bride's spotlight, Gabby later slipped into a simple red dress.

The couple honeymooned in Portofino, Italy, a fishing village on the Italian Riviera, and then launched their new life together. They spend most of their time in the ultramodern home they own in the Hollywood Hills,

Kimmel married Molly McNearney on July 13, 2013, in Ojai, California. At the ceremony, McNearney pranked Kimmel by getting another woman to stand in for her and walk down the aisle in a replica of her wedding dress.

but on weekends they stay at their four-bedroom beach house on Hermosa Beach. The house in the Hollywood Hills is the ultimate man cave. It has TVs everywhere. TVs in the bathrooms, one in the kitchen, four in the dining room, and one large-screen plasma set over the backyard grill. There are seventeen TVs in all. Kimmel can walk from room to room and never miss a moment of his favorite shows!

While the beach house is a bit more modest, both homes are well equipped with renovated kitchens because Kimmel loves to cook. On a trip to visit McNearney's family in St. Louis, Kimmel, an exacting foodie, discovered that his mother-in-law planned to cook a pasta dinner using tomato sauce from a jar, and he could not let that happen. He sprang into action, shopped for fresh ingredients to feed thirty people, and prepared a dish of penne marinara for his in-laws, their family, and friends. "I really am married to Martha Stewart," McNearney said.[4]

Heartfelt Plea

For Jimmy Kimmel, having a wedding wasn't just about celebrating the beginning of his new life with Molly McNearney—it was about scoring some household appliances. In his first show back since the wedding, he joked, "The reason I got married is I needed a panini maker and it seemed like the cheapest way to get it." The newlywed funnyman cracked several other wedding jokes throughout his monologue. He teased that he was shocked by the high cost of throwing a wedding. "First, you have to ship the bride in from Russia," he quipped.

"Then, there's the reception. You know how much 300 Lean Cuisine [frozen] dinners cost? A lot!"[5]

Three days before the couple celebrated their first wedding anniversary, they welcomed their first child, Jane, on July 10, 2014. A son, William, whom they call Billy, arrived on April 21, 2017. Kimmel's newborn son came into the world with a congenital heart defect that would require multiple surgeries. Billy was rushed to Children's Hospital of Los Angeles where he underwent a three-hour operation to repair a hole in his heart. The surgery was successful, and six days later, Billy came home. When Kimmel returned to his show the following week, he told viewers his infant son was doing well, though he would need another surgery in a few months. He then showed a photograph of Billy, one in

Fish Feast

Jimmy Kimmel loves to cook, and holidays bring out his best. Every year, he cooks a huge Christmas Eve feast for fifty family and friends that takes four days to prepare. He uses an old family recipe to make a fish stew called *cioppino*. His menu also includes raw clams and oysters, stone crab claws, skewered shrimp, scungilli salad, stuffed squid, lobster tail, linguine with lobster sauce, and a white fish called turbot. The annual Feast of Seven Fishes dinner extravaganza was inspired by Kimmel's childhood memories of his native Brooklyn. "I feel like I'm carrying on a family tradition," he said.[6]

Kimmel, holding son Billy, and wife, Molly, holding daughter Jane, helped raise more than $1.3 million to fight pediatric cancer at a fund raiser for Alex's Lemonade Stand Foundation in 2017.

● ●

the hospital with tubes sticking out of his body, and the other at home and smiling. "Poor kid, not only did he get a bad heart, he got my face," he said.[7]

Kimmel tried not to get emotional but failed as he talked tearfully about his son's open-heart surgery. He used his experience as the parent of a sick child to make an impassioned plea to US elected government officials to restore and improve funding for children's health insurance coverage. As he spoke, a phone number to Congress was flashed on the screen and viewers were urged to call their representative and get involved. His message was deeply personal. "If your baby is going to die and doesn't have to, it shouldn't matter how much money you make," he said. "No parent should ever have to decide if they can afford to save their child's life."[8]

The monologue quickly spread online and became a main focus of news media coverage. Due to his high profile, critics accused Kimmel of politicizing his son's heart defect. He was now thrust into the middle of the nation's health care debate. Kimmel took a swipe at his detractors and never once backed down from the cause he championed. The legislative bill that would have limited health care coverage for millions of Americans was defeated. More than any other pundit or politician, Kimmel received credit for his advocacy. A columnist wrote in the *New York Times*, "Mr. Kimmel's voice rang louder in the hubbub over healthcare than any politician's or any other comedian's."[9]

Later that year, a second heart operation was performed on eight-month-old Billy Kimmel. His father took a leave of absence while Billy recovered. Kimmel returned to his show on December 11, 2017, with Billy in his arms, and told the audience his son was "doing great" just one week after surgery. Billy stayed remarkably calm on camera as his father choked back tears. He then went on to thank the doctors at the hospital. "They say he's probably on track to win at least a bronze medal in the Olympics in 2036," Kimmel joked.[10]

> No parent should ever have to decide if they can afford to save their child's life.

Standing Oh

Jimmy Kimmel never expected to fill the role of America's conscience, but it only made sense that his focus began to shift more toward politics after the country elected a former reality star as president. When he hosted the Oscars in February 2017, Kimmel spent a good deal of his monologue going after the president for his overreaching and curious attack on Hollywood star Meryl Streep. Kimmel praised the Academy Award–winning actress's many "overrated performances," referencing one of the president's recent tweets. Kimmel joked Streep has "phoned it in for over 50 films in her lackluster career" and called on the audience to give her a "totally undeserved round of applause."[11]

Making Sense

Late-night comedy shows have long exploited issues that divide us to poke fun at our differences for easy laughs. Hosts such as Stephen Colbert, Seth Meyers, and Trevor Noah have brilliant, but scripted, takes on the national zeitgeist. They are commentators at arm's length from the issue. By contrast, Kimmel speaks from the heart. When he preached about preserving funding for children's health insurance, he spoke from personal experience, giving him a moral clarity the others can't muster. That's why his message packed a bracing wallop.

Kimmel never set out to be a moral arbiter, and he doesn't see himself in that role. But when a terrible, inexplicable, shocking, and painful tragedy occurs, his natural instinct is to tone down the jokes and use his platform to speak truth to power. He was visibly shaken following the mass shooting in his hometown of Las Vegas when a gunman in a high-rise hotel fired on a crowd at an outdoor concert in October 2017. He admonished Washington lawmakers for failing to take any meaningful action on gun control. Then he showed his audience pictures of 56 senators who voted against a bill to close loopholes that allow people to avoid a background check when buying guns privately. It was a moment that recalled legendary news anchor Walter Cronkite speaking out against the Vietnam War, which changed public opinion of the war.

In the space of just a few years, Jimmy Kimmel transformed himself from late night's average guy to a truth teller with a moral compass. He still likes fart jokes and a good phony phone call. He still loves to pull pranks on his friends, and colleagues—for years he sent out a Christmas card on behalf of his agent James Dixon that featured an oil painting of Dixon splayed naked on its cover—but when a serious issue has real-life implications, he is an effective and skillful communicator with a moral conscience. He isn't defined by politics but will address them head on when it becomes personal. "There are certain things I don't understand, and the idea that Americans wouldn't want to take care of each other when they're sick is one of them. The idea that our politicians would let the gun lobby tell them what to do is another."[12]

CHAPTER TEN

Renaissance Man

· ·

On November 13, 2017, Kimmel celebrated his fiftieth birthday on *Jimmy Kimmel Live!* Actor Ben Affleck and *Star Wars* director J. J. Abrams brought along with them the ultimate gift: a star-studded movie trailer based on *The Terrific Ten*, a comic book published by Kimmel Komix that he wrote when he was only ten years old. Abrams unveiled the surprise and delivered a nearly seven-minute trailer for the superhero flick, which the director joked cost $250 million to shoot.

Abrams recruited Affleck, Jennifer Aniston, Ty Burrell, Shaquille O'Neal, Will Arnett, Billy Crudup, Zach Galifianakis, Jon Hamm, and Jason Bateman to portray superheroes with ridiculous names you'd expect the mind of a ten-year-old boy to dream up: Color Kid, Muscle Man, Lucky Lad, and Super Duck, who was played by Galifianakis in a fowl costume, declaring, "Release the Quacken." Matt Damon, of course, played supervillain Dr. Bolt, along with Wanda Sykes as his sidekick, the Bleach Master, essentially her floating head inside a box of bleach. "The characters, they really spoke to me," Abrams told Kimmel before the trailer screened. "It demanded to be brought to life. I didn't change a word." Seeing the pages of his original comic book brought to life tickled the late-night host. "That was the best gift I ever got," he said.[1]

Street Smart Aleck

If you're not familiar with a new segment on *Jimmy Kimmel Live!* called "Lie Witness News," you're missing out on a fascinating and hilarious psychology

Jimmy Kimmel Live! merchandise is frequently donated to charities, such as one of Kimmel's favorite, the Feast of San Gennaro in Los Angeles, which celebrates Italian culture and raises funds to aid disadvantaged children and needy families in the city.

experiment. The premise is this: Kimmel's staff takes to the streets as roving reporters and questions pedestrians about recent events in the news. However, the events are fictitious, made up, not true, and usually ridiculous. Yet the reactions of the interviewees are fascinating. Without flinching, they always have an opinion on the matter, and somehow they've always heard the story from another source beforehand.

South by Southwest is a music festival known for providing a venue for indie artists. As part of his coverage of the annual Austin, Texas, festival in March 2015, Kimmel unveiled the "Lie Witness News" segment in which an interviewer asked SXSW festival goers if they liked a number of made-up bands. Surprisingly, several people claimed not only to have heard of the fake bands, but also truly enjoyed their music. One woman was a big fan of Wiz Khalifa's little brother, Cheese Wiz Khalifa, and claimed her friend was an even bigger fan. When quizzed about the music of French artist DJ Fictionelle, the same woman said she enjoyed the music and went so far as to claim she saw the fake musician when she was visiting Lyon, France.

Other groups included DJ Underwire; Eddie and His Man Purse; Mary Kate and Nasty, in a mashup on the names of Olsen twins Ashley and Mary Kate; and Vlad and the Putins, a twist on the name of the Russian president Vladimir Putin. One man was asked if he was a fan of DJ Gluten, even though "a lot of people say he's hard to tolerate." Apparently, the man had downloaded some of DJ Gluten's music to his phone.[2]

Fake News

Jimmy Kimmel tricked people into complaining about an awards show that never happened. For one "Lie Witness News" segment, people on the streets of Los Angeles were asked for their take on a fake event from the made-up broadcast of the Outstanding Celebrity Excellence Awards. Some random passersby didn't hesitate to confirm that they watched the nonexistent show. When a reporter asked how one woman felt about Tom Bergeron mansplaining women's reproductive rights, she replied, "Honestly, I was disgusted." Another had no problem voicing outrage at Alicia Keys for killing a ladybug that supposedly landed on her arm. "Stop killing ladybugs," the woman warned. "You may not believe in reincarnation, but other people do." Another suggested that instead of the hosts asking for applause by saying, "put your hands together," people should have been asked to "celebrate" so that those without hands would feel included.

Music Man

Music is an important element of variety shows, and Kimmel has a passion for bringing great artists to his show with the music-centric *Jimmy Kimmel Live!* Concert Series. This segment comprises a musical performance at the end of the show, which is performed on either an indoor or outdoor stage, or on location. Either way, he gives musicians and bands the biggest stage to rock out on. Fans are then given access to the complete performance via online streaming.

Kimmel is himself an accomplished musician. He plays the bass clarinet and played the instrument in his high school marching band. He was a guest performer at a February 29, 2008, concert at the Pearl Theater at the Palms, in Las Vegas, featuring the ska punk bank The Mighty Mighty Bosstones. Dicky Barrett is the front man of the band and the announcer for *Jimmy Kimmel Live!* He is known for his distinctively loud, gravelly voice. Toward the end of the show, Barrett stoked the crowd's enthusiasm when he announced that special guest "Licorice Jimmy" would be joining the band onstage for a song. A collective look of confusion passed over the faces of the crowd. Everyone cheered wildly when,

Kimmel plays bass clarinet and often is invited onstage as a guest performer with the ska punk bank the Mighty Mighty Bosstones. The band's front man, Dicky Barrett, is the announcer for *Jimmy Kimmel Live!*

much to their surprise, Kimmel stepped onstage with his enormous bass clarinet to offer backup on the Bosstones' best-known song, "The Impression That I Get."

Kimmel also plays harmonica. His BMW sport utility vehicle is full of harmonicas. Nearly a dozen of them are heaped in a pile in the center console and a case of harmonicas sits stashed on the back seat. He likes to play them while driving to work and says he gets a lot of weird looks from other drivers at stoplights. He's good at playing "Piano Man," according to his wife. During the 2016 presidential election campaign, Kimmel challenged Hillary Clinton's vice presidential running mate, Tim Kaine, to a debate at a Buffalo Wild Wings in Virginia. During the debate, Kimmel shared some of his plans for the country. For example, Americans deserve to have the Monday after the Super Bowl off from work. Kimmel also proposed that each citizen only post to social media twice daily and that concert attendees be seated in ascending height order. Kaine, a noted harmonica player, liked those ideas, and even though there wasn't much to argue, Kimmel said, "I think there's only one way for us to settle this. Harmonica battle."[3] Kaine proceeded to show off his impressive skills while Kimmel used the help of acclaimed harmonica master and Blues Traveler front man John Popper, hiding in a nearby booth as Kimmel mimed blowing a tune. The skit ended with a Kaine and Popper jam session.

Country Twang

One of Kimmel's most popular recurring bits is "Celebrities Read Mean Tweets." He searches the Twittersphere to find some of the more insulting things people have said about certain celebrities. Then he invites them to come on his show and read some tweets that people have posted about them. Following the Country Music Awards in November 2017, Kimmel brought a bunch of country music's biggest stars down a peg.

Blake Shelton, Darius Rucker, the Zac Brown Band, Chris Stapleton, Lady Antebellum, Little Big Town, and many others read harsh tweets about themselves. Some, like Blake Shelton, were able to laugh off their haters. Shelton added a slightly indignant tone to his mostly deadpan reading of someone's desire to throw

Top Tweets

The internet can be cruel. The popular *Jimmy Kimmel Live!* segment called "Celebrities Read Mean Tweets" is where famous stars come face-to-face with the most disparaging comments made about them online. The celebrities read the mean tweets and react on camera. Here are a few online critiques that were read by the celebrity being dissed.

- "Barack Obama is the Nickelback of presidents."
- "Selena Gomez is on the radio right now. Is there a volume lower than mute?"
- "Jim Parsons looks like a ventriloquist dummy that came to life."
- "Dear God, give us Tupac [Shakur] back and we'll give you Justin Bieber."
- "Melissa McCarthy is the Madea of white people."

> "This job is a grind, and best-case scenario, a marathon."

him "off a highway overpass by his legs and watch him get obliterated by a Peterbilt [heavy-duty truck] pulling a big stupid house."

Meanwhile, Stapleton got a laugh out of the suggestion that he's proof "ugly people can still win awards." Later, CMA's winner as vocal group of the year Little Big Town reacted with a mixture of horror and chuckles at the notion that they "sound like they threw a bunch of cats in a bag and beat them with a tennis racquet."[4]

Fade to Black

Jimmy Kimmel has spent seventy hours a week toiling away on his ABC late-night talk show since 2003. He rewrites his own monologues and extensively researches guests. But Kimmel has thought about retiring from the show that turned him into a household name when his contract expires in the fall of 2019. At a certain point, he'd like to have a little more free time. As the executive producer of his show and self-described control freak, he arrives at his Hollywood studios at 9 a.m., shoots at around 5 p.m., and returns to his computer after dinner to write jokes. "This job is a grind, and best-case scenario, a marathon," he said.[5]

Jimmy Kimmel Live! has received Emmy nominations for Outstanding Variety Series every year since 2012. Whenever retirement day arrives, audiences will miss his signature stunts. Some are harmless and goofy, like

Kimmel's sensitive and nurturing side is evident whenever he speaks out for causes that are important to him.

• • • • • • • • • • • • • • • • • • • •

the time he festooned actor John Krasinski's house with eight truckloads of Christmas decorations. Some are revelatory, like street interviews asking people whether they prefer the Affordable Care Act or its euphemism, Obamacare (many denounced the former while praising the latter), and interviewing people who lie about having watched the fifth quarter of the Super Bowl (football games are four quarters). Other pranks are just diabolical nonsense, like posting a video of a young woman twerking until she falls on a candle and catches on fire. That video went viral, getting nearly 23 million hits, before Kimmel admitted it was a hoax. When asked what he hoped to accomplish from such a stunt, he said, "Hopefully put an end to twerking forever."[6]

Jimmy Kimmel, America salutes you.

Chronology

1967 On November 13, James Christian Kimmel is born in Brooklyn, New York.

1977 Kimmel moves with his family to Las Vegas, Nevada.

1982 On February 1, *Late Night with David Letterman* makes its debut on NBC.

1985 While still in high school, Kimmel begins broadcasting at the college radio station KUNV in Las Vegas. Kimmel enrolls at the University of Nevada at Las Vegas.

1986 Kimmel's family moves to Phoenix, Arizona. Kimmel enrolls at Arizona State University in Tempe.

1988 On June 25, Kimmel, age twenty, marries college sweetheart Gina Maddy.

1989 Kimmel drops out of Arizona State and lands his first paying radio job at KZOK-FM in Seattle, Washington.

1991 Daughter Katie is born on August 28.

1992 Kimmel is hired by KCMJ-AM in Palm Springs, California, and hires Carson Daly as his intern.

1993 Son Kevin is born on September 19.

1994 After a series of radio jobs, Kimmel is hired at KROQ-FM in Los Angeles, finding much-needed stability.

1997 Kimmel is hired to cohost Comedy Central's game show *Win Ben Stein's Money*.

1999 Kimmel wins a Daytime Emmy Award for Outstanding Game Show Host; on June 16, *The Man Show* starring Kimmel and Adam Carolla premieres on Comedy Central; Kimmel becomes known to football fans as "Jimmy the Fox Guy" predicting the results of games on Fox's Sunday NFL pregame show.

2002 Kimmel's production company Jackhole Industries creates a popular puppet show called *Crank Yankers* on Comedy Central.

2003 On January 26, ABC's new late-night show *Jimmy Kimmel Live!* debuts in the midnight timeslot; in June, Kimmel and wife Gina divorce, ending their fourteen-year marriage; in August, Kimmel goes public about his narcolepsy in an article in *Esquire* magazine.

2007 In October, Kimmel earns a Guinness World Record for traveling 22,406 miles in a single week for work.

2009 In March, Kimmel and girlfriend Sarah Silverman amicably end their relationship.

2011 In August, Kimmel delivers an emotional tribute to his uncle, Frank Potenza, who dies at seventy-seven.

2012 On September 23, Kimmel hosts the 64th Primetime Emmy Awards; on October 31, he interviews his idol, David Letterman, for the first time.

2013 On January 8, *Jimmy Kimmel Live!* debuts in its new 11:35 p.m. timeslot; on January 25, Kimmel receives a star on Hollywood Boulevard's Walk of Fame; on May 19, the University of Nevada at Las Vegas awards Kimmel an honorary doctorate for his television and comedic success; on July 13, Kimmel marries coworker Molly McNearney in Ojai, California.

2014 On July 10, daughter Jane is born.

2016 On September 18, Kimmel hosts the 68th Primetime Emmy Awards; it is his second time as host.

2017 On February 26, Kimmel hosts the 89th Academy Awards; son Billy is born on April 21; Kimmel delivers an emotional monologue about controlling health care costs following his son's emergency open-heart surgery; on October 2, Kimmel delivers another tearful monologue about gun control following a mass shooting in his hometown of Las Vegas; on December 11, Kimmel appears on his show with son Billy following the child's second heart operation.

2018 On March 4, Kimmel hosts the 90th Academy Awards; it is his second time as host.

Chapter Notes

Chapter One: Brooklyn Boy

1. Stephanie Hockridge, "Jimmy Kimmel: Parents Reflect on the early years," Scripps Media, Inc., February 7, 2013, https://www.abc15.com/news/region-southeast-valley/tempe/jimmy-kimmel-parents-reflect-on-the-early-years.

2. *Fresh Air* with Terry Gross, "Jimmy Kimmel: Making Late Night a Family Affair," National Public Radio, January 23, 2013, https://www.npr.org/2013/01/23/168808769/jimmy-kimmel-making-late-night-a-family-affair.

3. Ibid.

4. Bill Carter, "Frank Potenza, Foil for Kimmel, Is Dead at 77," *New York Times*, August 26, 2011, http://www.nytimes.com/2011/08/26/arts/television/frank-potenza-foil-for-nephew-jimmy-kimmel-dies-at-77.html.

5. Erin Durkin, "Jimmy Kimmel to Return to Native Brooklyn for Week of Shows in October," *New York Daily News*, May 14, 2012, http://www.nydailynews.com/entertainment/tv-movies/jimmy-kimmel-return-native-brooklyn-week-shows-october-article-1.1077946.

6. Joe Satran, "Jimmy Kimmel, Emmy Host, Rose from Beer-Drinking Bozo to America's Favorite Emcee,"

Huffington Post, September 21, 2012, https://www
.huffingtonpost.com/2012/09/21/jimmy-kimmel-
emmy_n_1901978.html.

Chapter Two: Kimmel's Big Move

1. Michael Paterniti, "Jimmy Kimmel Is Seriously Funny,"
   GQ, January 16, 2018, https://www.gq.com/story/
   jimmy-kimmel-is-seriously-funny.

2. Elias Leight, "See Ben Affleck, Matt Damon Bring
   Jimmy Kimmel's Childhood Comic to Life," *Rolling
   Stone*, November 14, 2017, https://www.rollingstone
   .com/tv/news/affleck-damon-bring-jimmy-kimmels-
   childhood-comic-to-life-w511701.

3. Mick Stingley, "Jimmy Kimmel Shares Childhood
   Stories Growing Up in Las Vegas," *ABC News*, October
   4, 2017, http://abcnews.go.com/Entertainment/
   jimmy-kimmel-shares-childhood-stories-growing-las-
   vegas/story?id=50275073.

4. Geoff Edgers, "David Letterman's Friends—and
   Shrink—Make His Twain Ceremony as Funny as
   His Late-Night Legacy," *Washington Post*, October
   23, 2017, https://www.washingtonpost.com/lifestyle/
   style/david-lettermans-friends--and-shrink--make-
   his-twain-ceremony-as-funny-as-his-late-night-
   legacy/2017/10/23/b4f5a816-b79b-11e7-be94-
   fabb0f1e9ffb_story.html?utm_term=.4cbaaa4cf1a9.

5. Joe Satran, "Jimmy Kimmel, Emmy Host, Rose from
   Beer-Drinking Bozo to America's Favorite Emcee,"
   Huffington Post, September 21, 2012, https://www
   .huffingtonpost.com/2012/09/21/jimmy-kimmel-
   emmy_n_1901978.html.

6. Bill Carter, "In the Land of the Insomniac, the Narcoleptic Wants to Be King," *New York Times Magazine*, November 3, 2002, http://www.nytimes.com/2002/11/03/magazine/in-the-land-of-the-insomniac-the-narcoleptic-wants-to-be-king.html.

7. John Katsilometes, "Jimmy Kimmel Shows His Rebel Roots," *Vegas*, October 16, 2013, https://vegasmagazine.com/jimmy-kimmel-shows-his-rebel-roots.

Chapter Three: Merry Prankster

1. Joe Satran, "Jimmy Kimmel, Emmy Host, Rose from Beer-Drinking Bozo to America's Favorite Emcee," *Huffington Post*, September 21, 2012, https://www.huffingtonpost.com/2012/09/21/jimmy-kimmel-emmy_n_1901978.html.

2. Joe Rhodes, "Distilling the Fun from Dysfunctional," *New York Times*, October 21, 2007, http://www.nytimes.com/2007/10/21/arts/television/21rhod.html.

3. Kristine Cannon, "Jill Bryan on Big Bro Jimmy Kimmel and More," SheKnows.com, December 17, 2013, http://www.sheknows.com/entertainment.

4. "The Funniest Jimmy Kimmel Prank Ever," *ABC News*, April 2, 2015, http://abc7.com/entertainment/prank-madness-championship-vote-for-the-funniest-jimmy-kimmel-prank/616571/.

5. Stephanie Hockridge, "Jimmy Kimmel: Parents Reflect on the Early Years," Scripps Media, Inc., February 7, 2013, https://www.abc15.com/news/region-southeast-valley/tempe/jimmy-kimmel-parents-reflect-on-the-early-years.

6. Satran, "Jimmy Kimmel, Emmy Host, Rose from Beer-Drinking Bozo to America's Favorite Emcee."

7. "Jimmy Kimmel: The Hardest-Working Man in Show Business," *Success*, July 6, 2014, https://www.success .com/article/jimmy-kimmel-the-hardest-working-man-in-show-business.

8. Ibid.

9. Stephanie Hockridge, "Jimmy Kimmel: Parents Reflect on the Early Years."

10. Satran, "Jimmy Kimmel, Emmy Host, Rose from Beer-Drinking Bozo to America's Favorite Emcee."

11. Tim Gray, "Jimmy Kimmel on His First Hollywood Job and How He Got into TV," *Variety*, September 16, 2016, http://variety.com/2016/tv/awards/emmy-host-jimmy-kimmel-1201859652/.

12. "Jimmy Kimmel: The Hardest-Working Man in Dhow Business," *Success*.

13. Michael Paterniti, "Jimmy Kimmel Is Seriously Funny," *GQ*, January 16, 2018, https://www.gq.com/ story/jimmy-kimmel-is-seriously-funny.

Chapter Four: On the Road

1. Rick Kaempfer, "Chicago Radio Spotlight: Kent Voss," January 24, 2009, http://chicagoradiospotlight .blogspot.com/2009/01/kent-voss.html.

2. Joe Satran, "Jimmy Kimmel, Emmy Host, Rose from Beer-Drinking Bozo to America's Favorite Emcee," *Huffington Post*, September 21, 2012, https://www .huffingtonpost.com/2012/09/21/jimmy-kimmel-emmy_n_1901978.html.

3. Stephanie Hockridge, "Jimmy Kimmel's Parents: Stories You've Never Heard About His Rise to the Top," Scripps Media, Inc., February 24, 2013, https://www.abc15.com/news/region-southeast-valley/tempe/jimmy-kimmels-parents-the-stories-youve-never-heard-about-his-rise-to-the-top.

4. Satran, "Jimmy Kimmel, Emmy host, Rose from Beer-Drinking Bozo to America's Favorite Emcee."

5. "Jimmy Kimmel: The Hardest-Working Man in Show Business," *Success*, July 6, 2014, https://www.success.com/article/jimmy-kimmel-the-hardest-working-man-in-show-business.

6. Michael Paterniti, "Jimmy Kimmel Is Seriously Funny," *GQ*, January 16, 2018, https://www.gq.com/story/jimmy-kimmel-is-seriously-funny.

7. *The Meredith Vieira Show*, "Carson Daly on Jimmy Kimmel Being His Boss," January 22, 2015, https://www.youtube.com/watch?v=5i-8WnCHK5Q.

8. John Katsilometes, "Jimmy Kimmel a Fitting Ambassador for Las Vegas," *Las Vegas Sun*, October 30, 2013, https://lasvegassun.com/blogs/kats-report/2013/oct/30/jimmy-kimmel-fitting-ambassador-las-vegas/.

9. Satran, "Jimmy Kimmel, Emmy host, Rose from Beer-Drinking Bozo to America's Favorite Emcee."

Chapter Five: Kimmel's Big Break

1. Stuart Levine, "Ben Stein Reflects on Kimmel's 'Money' Days," *Variety*, January 25, 2013, http://variety.com/2013/tv/news/ben-stein-reflects-on-kimmel-s-money-days-1118065014/.

2. Joe Satran, "Jimmy Kimmel, Emmy Host, Rose from Beer-Drinking Bozo to America's Favorite Emcee," *Huffington Post*, September 21, 2012, https://www.huffingtonpost.com/2012/09/21/jimmy-kimmel-emmy_n_1901978.html.

3. Ibid.

4. Ibid.

5. Terry Kelleher, "Picks and Pans Reviews: *The Man Show*," *People*, June 28, 1999, http://people.com/archive/picks-and-pans-review-the-man-show-vol-51-no-24/.

6. Matt Springer, "TV Review: *The Man Show*," Common Sense Media, June 1999, https://www.commonsensemedia.org/tv-reviews/the-man-show.

Chapter Six: A Dream Comes True

1. Joe Satran, "Jimmy Kimmel, Emmy Host, Rose from Beer-Drinking Bozo to America's Favorite Emcee," *Huffington Post*, September 21, 2012, https://www.huffingtonpost.com/2012/09/21/jimmy-kimmel-emmy_n_1901978.html.

2. Bill Carter, "In the Land of the Insomniac, the Narcoleptic Wants to Be King," *New York Times Magazine*, November 3, 2002, http://www.nytimes.com/2002/11/03/magazine/in-the-land-of-the-insomniac-the-narcoleptic-wants-to-be-king.html.

3. Jonah Weiner, "Here's Jimmy Kimmel," *Rolling Stone*, March 1, 2013, https://www.rollingstone.com/movies/news/heres-jimmy-kimmel-20130301.

4. Noel Murray, "Jimmy Kimmel Interview," *The A.V. Club*, January 31, 2007, https://film.avclub.com/jimmy-kimmel-1798210737.

5. *People* staff, "Funniest Couple Alive," *People*, March 17, 2008, http://people.com/archive/funniest-couple-alive-vol-69-no-10/.

6. *Access Online*, "Jimmy Kimmel Talks Sarah Silverman Breakup on *The View*," NBC Universal, March 9, 2008, http://www.accessonline.com/articles/jimmy-kimmel-talks-sarah-silverman-break-up-on-the-view-68552/.

7. Jimmy Kimmel, as told to Brendan Vaughan, "What It Feels Like to Have Narcolepsy," *Esquire*, August 2003, http://jimmykimmel.net/articles/esquire0803.htm.

Chapter Seven: Kimmel Hits the Big Time

1. Nancy Franklin, "Boy Talk," *New Yorker*, March 17, 2003, https://www.newyorker.com/magazine/2003/03/17/boy-talk.

2. "Jimmy Kimmel Cries Over Uncle Frank Memories," ABC News, September 6, 2011, http://abcnews.go.com/Entertainment/video/jimmy-kimmel-cries-over-uncle-frank-memories-14462591.

3. YouTube, "YouTube Challenge: I Told My Kids I Ate All Their Halloween Candy 2017," November 2, 2017, https://www.youtube.com/watch?time_continue=36&v=bmCOjcaiXQM.

4. Tom Chiarella, "Kimmel Is the Jimmy!" *Esquire*, March 20, 2014, https://www.esquire.com/entertainment/tv/interviews/a32843/jimmy-kimmel-interview-0414/.

Chapter Eight: Kimmel Goes Viral

1. Peter Kafka, "Jimmy Kimmel on Fake Viral Videos, Real Money and the Future of TV," *Recode*, March 11, 2014, https://www.recode.net/2014/3/11/11624374/jimmy-kimmel-on-fake-viral-videos-real-money-and-the-future-of-tv.

2. YouTube, "F*@#ing Ben Affleck," January 16, 2009, https://www.youtube.com/watch?v=TwIyLHsk2h4.

3. YouTube, "Jimmy Kimmel's Oscars Monologue," February 26, 2017, https://www.youtube.com/watch?v=fDkXHWMNNmc.

4. YouTube, "Jimmy Kimmel's Tribute to Matt Damon at the Oscars," February 26, 2017, https://www.youtube.com/watch?v=PkjLMWS3U4Q.

5. YouTube, "Jimmy Kimmel Roasting at the 2012 White House Correspondents' Dinner," April 29, 2012, https://www.youtube.com/watch?v=l0CJsahneek.

6. *Fresh Air* with Terry Gross, "Jimmy Kimmel: Making Late Night a Family Affair," National Public Radio, January 23, 2013, https://www.npr.org/2013/01/23/168808769/jimmy-kimmel-making-late-night-a-family-affair.

7. Kevin Fallon, "Jimmy Kimmel Will Host Oscars: A Boring, Perfect Choice," *Daily Beast*, December 5, 2016, https://www.thedailybeast.com/jimmy-kimmel-will-host-the-oscars-a-boring-perfect-choice.

8. Chuck Barney, "Oscars Screw-up Aside, Jimmy Kimmel Shined as Academy Awards Host," *Mercury News*, February 26, 2017, https://www.mercurynews.com/2017/02/26/oscars-2017-how-is-jimmy-kimmel-doing/.

9. Tim Nudd, "Jimmy Kimmel Realizes Dream of Interviewing His Idol, David Letterman," *People*, November 1, 2012, http://people.com/tv/david-letterman-visits-jimmy-kimmel-show/.

10. YouTube, "Jennifer Aniston Destroys Jimmy Kimmel's New Set," January 19, 2013, https://www.youtube.com/watch?v=iAlj1ctdDYM.

Chapter Nine: A New Leaf

1. Sandy Cohen, "Jimmy Kimmel's Coast-to-Coast commute," *Washington Post*, October 15, 2007, http://www.washingtonpost.com/wp-dyn/content/article/2007/10/14/AR2007101401175.html.

2. Jonah Weiner, "Here's Jimmy Kimmel," *Rolling Stone*, March 1, 2013, https://www.rollingstone.com/movies/news/heres-jimmy-kimmel-20130301.

3. Jessica Radloff, "Molly McNearney Reveals How She Fell in Love with Jimmy Kimmel," *Glamour*, February 18, 2014, https://www.glamour.com/story/molly-mcnearney-reveals-how-sh.

4. Ibid.

5. "Jimmy Kimmel's Italian Christmas Eve," *People*, November 15, 2007, http://people.com/celebrity/jimmy-kimmels-italian-christmas-eve/.

6. Justin Harp, "Jimmy Kimmel on Wedding: I Needed a Cheap Way to Get Panini Maker," *Heart Magazines' Digital Spy*, July 30, 2013, http://www.digitalspy.com/showbiz/news/a502498/jimmy-kimmel-on-wedding-i-needed-a-cheap-way-to-get-panini-maker/.

7. YouTube, "Jimmy Kimmel Reveals Details of His Son's Birth & Heart Disease," May 1, 2017, https://www.youtube.com/watch?v=MmWWoMcGmo0.

8. Ibid.

9. Sandy Kenyon, "Jimmy Kimmel Brings 'Jimmy Kimmel Live!' to Brooklyn," WABC *Eyewitness News*, October 16, 2017, http://abc7ny.com/entertainment/jimmy-kimmel-brings-jimmy-kimmel-live-to-brooklyn/2538918/.

10. YouTube, "Jimmy Kimmel Returns with Baby Billy After Heart Surgery," December 11, 2017, https://www.youtube.com/watch?v=yqulWPljawo.

11. YouTube, "Jimmy Kimmel's Oscars Monologue," February 26, 2017, https://www.youtube.com/watch?v=fDkXHWMNNmc.

12. David Marchese, "In Conversation: Jimmy Kimmel," *Vulture*, October 29, 2017, http://www.vulture.com/2017/10/jimmy-kimmel-on-healthcare-trump-gun-control.html.

Chapter Ten: Renaissance Man

1. YouTube, "World Premiere Trailer: Jimmy Kimmel's *The Terrific Ten*," November 13, 2017, https://www.youtube.com/watch?v=t8Jq6NqCQ1o.

2. YouTube, "Lie Witness News, SXSW 2015," March 18, 2015, https://www.youtube.com/watch?v=lAVrryvHhk8.

3. YouTube, "Vice to Vice: Jimmy Kimmel vs. Tim Kaine," September 26, 2016, https://www.youtube.com/watch?v=HrOeglGQXo8.

4. YouTube, "Mean Tweets: Country Music Rendition #3," November 8, 2017, https://www.youtube.com/watch?v=k29YnfttqEU.

5. Ramin Setoodeh, "Jimmy Kimmel Is Considering Retiring from Late-Night TV," *Variety*, February 21, 2017, http://variety.com/2017/tv/news/jimmy-kimmel-considers-retiring-late-night-jimmy-kimmel-live-1201992589/.

6. YouTube, "Jimmy Kimmel Reveals 'Worst Twerk Fail Ever, Girl Catches Fire Prank," September 19, 2013, https://www.youtube.com/watch?v=HSJMoH7tnvw.

Glossary

Academy Awards Prestigious awards, casually called Oscars, presented in various categories for achievement in the movie industry. Given annually since 1928 from the Academy of Motion Picture Arts and Sciences in Hollywood, California.

caricature An exaggerated picture, description, or imitation of a person using unique and striking characteristics in order to create a comic effect.

demographic A particular and measurable sector of a population.

Emmy Awards Awards that recognize excellence in the television industry; TV equivalent to the Academy Awards.

euphemism A milder, more polite word or expression substituted to mask something unpleasant.

incorrigible Describes a person not able to be corrected, improved, or reformed.

luminary A person who inspires and influences others, especially one prominent in a particular field.

misogynistic Strongly prejudiced against women.

pantheon A collection of gods.

protégé A person who is guided and supported by an older, more experienced mentor.

pugnacious Eager or quick to argue, quarrel, or fight.

sonogram A visual image of a fetus produced from an ultrasound examination.

tenement A rundown and overcrowded apartment house, located in a poor section of a large city.

valedictorian A student having the highest academic achievements of the class, who delivers the valedictory at a graduation ceremony.

zeitgeist The defining spirit or mood of a particular period of history as shown by the ideas and beliefs of the time.

Further Reading

Books

Aldridge, Rebecca. *Stephen Colbert*. New York, NY: Rosen Publishing, 2016.

Carter, Bill. *The War for Late Night: When Leno Went Early and Television Went Crazy*. New York, NY: Viking, 2010.

Klein, Rebecca T. *Jimmy Fallon*. New York, NY: Rosen Publishing, 2016.

Zinoman, Jason. *Letterman: The Last Giant of Late Night*. New York, NY: HarperCollins, 2017.

Websites

Jimmy Kimmel Live!

http://abc.go.com/shows/jimmy-kimmel-live
The show's official website. Home of "Mean Tweets," "Lie Witness News," and "Unnecessary Censorship."

Jimmy Kimmel Live!—YouTube

https://www.youtube.com/user/JimmyKimmelLive
The official Jimmy Kimmel Live! YouTube Channel has all the favorite viral late-night videos.

Films

Jimmy Kimmel's Big Night of Stars. Director, Wayne McClammy. Jackhole Industries, 2008.

Windy City Heat. Director, Bobcat Goldthwait. Paramount Home Video, 2006.

Index